TEACHING TO
TRANSFORM
NOT INFORM

Volume 2

Resources by Dr. W. Bradley Simon

1. TEACHING TO TRANSFORM NOT INFORM 1:
Foundational Principles for Making an Informational
Sunday School Lesson...TRANSFORMATIONAL

2. DVD Video Companion for TEACHING TO
TRANSFORM NOT INFORM 1: Foundational Principles for
Making an Informational Sunday School
Lesson...TRANSFORMATIONAL

3. TEACHING TO TRANSFORM NOT INFORM 2:
How to Teach a Transformational Sunday
School Lesson...STEP-BY-STEP

4. DVD Video Companion for TEACHING
TO TRANSFORM NOT INFORM 2: How to
Teach a Transformational Sunday School
Lesson...STEP-BY-STEP

When purchasing books for a group,
see the www.M2820.com store for
bulk pricing.

Additional Resources

If you are training your teachers to craft and teach,
high-impact, life-altering lessons, visit our website for
additional resources (www.M2820.com).

TEACHING TO
TRANSFORM
NOT INFORM
VOLUME 2

How to Teach a Transformational
Sunday School Lesson…
STEP-BY-STEP

W. BRADLEY SIMON, PH.D.

28:20
TEACHING TO TRANSFORM
www.M2820.com

For additional companion teaching resources for this book or copyright inquires:

M28:20 M28:20, Bluffton, SC 29910
TEACHING TO TRANSFORM   www.M2820.com, info@M2820.com

Printed in the United States of America

All Scripture quotations, unless otherwise noted, are taken from The Holy Bible, New International Version®. NIV®. Copyright © 1973, 1978, 1984, 2011 by Biblica, Inc.™ Used by permission. All rights reserved worldwide. www.zondervan.com

Scripture quotations in italics or bold have been added by the author for emphasis.

Simon, W. Bradley, 1962–
Teaching to TRANSFORM Not Inform 2: How to Teach a Transformational Sunday School Lesson...STEP-BY-STEP (Sunday School Teacher Training)

ISBN 978-1-939257-21-5 (paperback)
Subject Headings: Christian education—Teacher training. 2. Sunday schools — Teaching methods. 3. Sunday schools — Teacher training.

Cover design by Bill Foster and Dr. W. Bradley Simon
Interior design by Dr. W. Bradley Simon

*Then Jesus came to them and said, "All authority in heaven and on earth has been given to me. Therefore go and make disciples of all nations, baptizing them in the name of the Father and of the Son and of the Holy Spirit, and **teaching them to obey** everything I have commanded you. And surely I am with you always, to the very end of the age."*

— Matthew 28:18-20

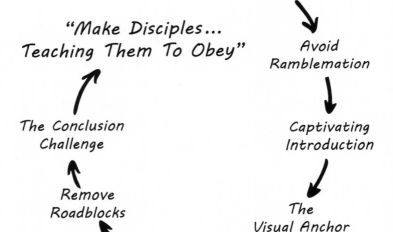

Table of Contents

Chapter Outlines

Ch: 3–Avoid Ramblemation

Transform lives with lessons
focused on and centered around the Sticky Proverb

Ch: 4–Captivating Introduction

Instantly grab and hold attention by showing
listeners your lesson's application and relevance

Cʜ: 5–The Visual Anchor

Create a lesson listeners will remember
for five or ten years . . . maybe a lifetime

Ch: 6–Here's-How Teaching

Teach lessons listeners can apply

B. Include that which directly supports the Sticky Proverb

Cʜ: 7–Remove Roadblocks

Lead listeners around
the obstacles that hinder their growth

A. Most truths make it onto the Scratchpad; fewer make it into the heart

B. Placing truth onto the Scratchpad is easy; transferring it to the heart is hard

A. For informational teachers, "No"

B. For M28:20 transformational teachers, "Yes!"

A. Identify what the Bible is asking listeners to change

1. *List changes related to the head*

2. *List changes related to the heart*

3. *List changes related to the hands*

B. Identify roadblocks that may impede this change

1. *Identify roadblocks during your preparation time*

2. *Focus on gray areas people struggle with rather than black-and-white generalities*

3. *Identify additional roadblocks during the lesson*

C. Determine how to biblically remove each roadblock

Ch: 8–The Conclusion Challenge

Encourage life-change by concluding
with a clear, specific, doable challenge

Introduction

In Matthew 28:19–20, Jesus gives teachers a clear and concise teaching goal: *"Therefore go and make disciples... teaching them to obey everything I have commanded you."* He does not say, teach people *what* to obey or even *how* to obey; rather, Jesus says, *"make disciples... teaching them to obey."* As a result, Jesus makes life-altering transformation (not simply information or explanation) our primary teaching goal.

Consequently, the *Teaching to TRANSFORM Not Inform* series focuses on showing you how to turn informationally or educationally oriented Bible lessons into life-altering transformational ones. You will learn how to teach not only the head but also the heart which results in changed lives. You will learn how to integrate transformational principles throughout your teaching so you can fulfill the Great Commission as a Bible teacher.

In the first book in this series, *Teaching to TRANSFORM Not Inform 1: Foundational Principles for Making an Informational Sunday School Lesson...Transformational,* you will discover the biblical principles, attitudes, priorities, and goals that will help you maximize your impact as a teacher. As you work through additional books in this series, they will build upon previous ones giving you a linear path for developing more and more advanced teaching skills. For example, this second book, builds upon the foundation presented in the first book and gives you a simple, practical, step-by-step process for how to develop and teach a Bible lesson that changes hearts and transforms lives.

1

The Seven Ingredients

The seven ingredients that make a Bible study more transformational than informational

*Do your best
to present yourself to God
as one approved, a workman
who does not need to be ashamed and
who correctly handles the word of truth.*

— 2 Timothy 2:15

SPOTTING A TRANSFORMATIONAL TEACHER is fairly easy to do. Amongst other things, they quickly gain and hold attention, clearly explain the text, help listeners remove internal roadblocks, and then challenge them to accept and apply the truth to their lives. As a result, listeners' beliefs, thoughts, attitudes, hopes, dreams, priorities, values, and actions change over time. It is no wonder why God considers their ministry within the church to be of vital importance. Look at what Paul tells us in Ephesians:

> It was he who gave some to be apostles, some to be prophets, some to be evangelists, and some to be pastors and teachers, to prepare God's people for works of service, so that the body of Christ may be built up until we all reach unity in the faith and in the knowledge of the Son of God and become mature, attaining to the whole measure of the fullness of Christ.
>
> — Ephesians 4:11–13

Even though spotting a transformational teacher is fairly easy to do, becoming one is more difficult because it involves integrating several different teaching principles at the same time. For the casual observer, the teaching process appears to be straightforward: people come in, sit down, listen to some inspirational teaching, leave, and have their lives changed over time. Seems simple enough. However, what they don't realize is the simpler the lesson appears and the more impact it has in people's lives, the more skillfully the teacher has integrated teaching principles throughout the entire lesson. When done correctly, teaching principles are invisible and the lesson just works. When done incorrectly, the teaching process comes to a grinding halt.

Let's look at a common example. Have you ever noticed how some teachers can ask a question and everyone just sits there? Answers are given, but often just to alleviate the awkward silence. On the other hand, other teachers can ask a question, and it is difficult to get a word in edgewise because everyone is trying to give their opinion.

What makes the difference? Why did one teacher's question result in an awkward silence while the other sparked a ten-minute discussion? It all comes back to the teacher's ability to integrate teaching principles invisibly and effectively. Few, if any, probably noticed how the teacher directed the class discussion to prepare them for the upcoming, carefully crafted question. The class just assumed everyone was talkative that day. Everyone experienced the effect, but few realized the cause. To fully understand how it happened, you usually can't just watch the teacher in action; rather, most of the time, you need someone to point out what the teacher did, why it was done, and how it affected listeners.

And, of course, that is the goal of this series of seminars: to point out some of the most effective teaching principles you can use, why and when you should use them, and how they will impact your listeners. Within this book, we will look at the goal and purpose of seven of the most important teaching principles you should include in every lesson. In advanced books/seminars, we will discuss additional teaching principles along with methods and techniques you can use to integrate them into your lesson. The seven principles we will cover in the following chapters are as follows:

1. **Sticky Proverb:** A short, memorable proverb that clearly states the passage's central truth and application.
2. **Ramblemation:** Transform lives with lessons focused on and centered around the Sticky Proverb.
3. **Captivating Introduction:** Instantly grab and hold attention by connecting listeners to the lesson's application and relevance.
4. **Visual Anchor:** The visual, concrete image, object, story, illustration, analogy, example, metaphor, testimony, or real-life situation that depicts the lesson's Sticky Proverb in a ridiculous, crazy, impossible, illogical, absurd, disproportionate, exaggerated, or animated way.
5. **Here's-How Teaching:** The thorough, applicable explanation of the biblical text that directly supports the Sticky Proverb.

6. **Roadblocks:** The challenges, experiences, misunderstandings, justifications, rationalizations, and objections the teacher helps listeners remove so they can integrate the truth into their life.

7. **The Conclusion Challenge:** Summary of the most important points and the challenge to apply them.

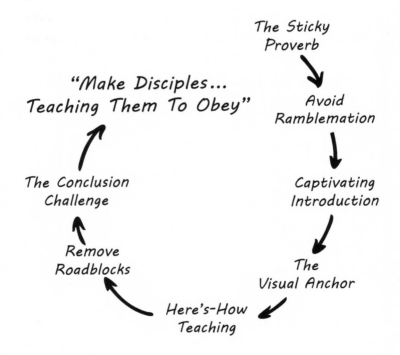

The Sticky Proverb

"Make Disciples... Teaching Them To Obey"

Avoid Ramblemation

The Conclusion Challenge

Captivating Introduction

Remove Roadblocks

The Visual Anchor

Here's-How Teaching

Leading a teacher training seminar?

If you believe the teachers within your church would benefit from the *Teaching to TRANSFORM Not Inform* series, consider leading them in a study using the books within the series. See the store at www.M2820.com for bulk pricing.

Another possibility includes hosting a live *Teaching to TRANSFORM Not Inform* conference at your church. Our goal is to train teachers to fulfill the Great Commission through their teaching ministry at no cost to your church or organization. This is possible when a few different churches participate in the training. To see how this works, see our website or call the number listed on our website.

2

The Sticky Proverb

Help listeners live godly lives
by presenting practical, memorable, life-principles

*It was he who gave some to be ... pastors
and teachers, to prepare God's people
for works of service, so that the body of
Christ may be built up.*

—Ephesians 4:11–12

Chapter Outline / Notes

I. **Craft a Sticky Proverb for every lesson**

   A. Create a short, memorable proverbial statement that reveals how to apply the lesson's primary truth

   B. Example: "Before you do it, look around"

II. **Advantages of creating a Sticky Proverb**

   A. Helps your listeners:

      1. Understand why specific information is being presented

      2. Mentally organize the information

      3. Rejoin the lesson after a distraction

      4. Remember the lesson's central truth and application

B. Helps the teacher:

    1. Identify and clarify the lesson's teaching goal

    2. Articulate the passage's primary truth and principle

    3. Narrow the lesson's exact direction, angle, and focus

    4. Determine which verses need to be included or excluded

C. Prevents Ramblemation

III. Sticky Proverb examples:
A. The Golden Rule

B. The Trash Can

*O*NE OF LIFE'S GREATEST CHALLENGES IS knowing how to apply biblical truths and principles to situations as they arise. We aren't given time to study the Bible, look back through sermon notes, or read a good book on the subject; instead, we have to choose a solution or principle and apply it to the situation. Sometimes, we remember a related Sunday school lesson or sermon, but it is often difficult to remember its exact principles or conclusion.

Fortunately, we can help those within our class remember the conclusions we reach with the use of a Sticky Proverb. Few remember lengthy lessons or discussions, but most can remember a well-written proverb. With a proverb, we can condense an entire lesson into a short, pithy, practical statement that will stick in our listeners' memories until a situation arises requiring its wisdom and insights.

It is amazing how proverbs in general (spiritual or not) are passed down from generation to generation: from grandparents to parents to children. Some of these proverbs are uplifting and inspirational, while others admonish in a profound (rather than a spiteful or demoralizing) manner. Some clarify abstract truths, while others function as general guides to conduct. Still others are simply a commentary on human nature or behavior.

Below are just a few of the hundreds of proverbs we hear and use all the time. Are there times when you or your children would have profited from following the insights found in one of the following proverbs?

A bird in the hand is worth two in the bush.

A house divided against itself cannot stand.

A house is not a home.

A leopard cannot change its spots.

A penny saved is a penny earned.

A picture is worth a thousand words.

A soft answer turneth away wrath.

Actions speak louder than words.

Do not burn your bridges behind you.

Do not cast your pearls before swine.

Do not make a mountain of a mole hill.

Do not put all your eggs in one basket.

Failing to plan is planning to fail.

He who lives by the sword shall die by the sword.

Hindsight is always twenty-twenty.

Honesty is the best policy.

If life deals you lemons, make lemonade.

If you cannot stand the heat, get out of the kitchen.

It is better to give than to receive.

It is no use crying over spilt milk.

Look before you leap.

Never judge a book by its cover.

Never let the sun go down on your anger.

No man can serve two masters.

No pain, no gain.

Pride goes before a fall.

Put your best foot forward.

Spare the rod and spoil the child.

You cannot have your cake and eat it.

I. Craft a Sticky Proverb for every lesson

Most books on teaching, preaching, or speaking encourage the practice of creating a single short sentence that summarizes the lesson's central idea or main truth.

The exact goal and purpose of this summary sentence can vary from author to author, which is one of the reasons they give it slightly different names. Some of the more common names include the Big Idea, the Central Idea/Thought/Theme/Principle, the Propositional Statement, the Thesis Statement, the Exegetical Idea, the Take-Home Truth, or similarly, the Takeaway Point. Even though all these names are fine, none of them accurately describe the role or purpose I believe this teaching element should have, so I created the new name, the Sticky Proverb.

A. Create a short, memorable proverbial statement that reveals how to apply the lesson's primary truth

The Sticky Proverb is a summary sentence that states the central truth of the lesson in a single pithy statement. It gives the primary principle taught in the lesson. It expresses the core truth you want listeners to remember. It is the most important precept listeners need to apply.

When developing your lesson, it is best to first study the Bible passage. Then, before doing anything else, craft a "Sticky Proverb" for the lesson, that is, create a single, brief, memorable nugget of wisdom (or proverb) that reveals how listeners can apply the lesson's central truth or principle in today's culture.

It's sticky in the sense that it is easy to remember long after the conclusion of your message, and it's a proverb in the sense that it is a short sentence that reveals how the biblical principle can be applied in our 21st-century lives. It is a short, memorable sentence that reveals how the passage's overarching truth can be used to make daily decisions. It is a proverbial rule-of-thumb that helps listeners make biblical life choices.

---

*A Sticky Proverb is a
short, memorable, proverbial rule-of-thumb
that shows listeners how to use
biblical principles to make daily decisions.*

Once you develop this memorable statement, you will have a pretty good idea of what you want to achieve through the lesson and how you want it to affect your listeners. Once you know what your Sticky Proverb is going to be, you know what target you are aiming for as you create your title, outline, illustrations, and application.

So, the first step in preparing a lesson is to study the passage. Then, before doing anything else, create a Sticky Proverb. Finally, after you know which target you are aiming for, develop the rest of the lesson.

B. Example: "Before you do it, look around"

Even though we will look at a few examples of a Sticky Proverb later in this chapter, let's look at one now so we can get a better idea of what we're talking about. A few weeks ago, I taught a lesson on Romans 14:13–21. In this passage, Paul taught that it was morally acceptable to eat meat that had been offered to idols. However, he countered by saying that if eating such meat causes someone around you to fall into sin, it is no longer all right to eat it.

As a result, it seemed that the passage's timeless truth that applied to our lives today was that we should avoid publicly doing, saying, eating, drinking, attending, or participating in anything that might cause less-mature believers around us to fall into sin, even if those actions are morally acceptable.

So, before creating the lesson outline, I created a Sticky Proverb, that is, a brief, easy-to-remember proverb that reveals how this central truth can be applied in my listeners' lives. Here's what I came up with: "Before you do it, look around." In other words, before you publicly do, say, eat, drink, attend, or participate in anything that may be morally all right to do, first "look around" to make sure your actions won't cause someone watching you to fall into sin.

Now, you may be thinking to yourself, "Hmm, I'm sure you could improve your Sticky Proverb," and you would be right. Once you come up with your statement, there are a number of ways to make it stickier.

One way to add some additional stickiness is to replace abstract words or concepts with symbolic word pictures. For example, let's say you were creating a Sticky Proverb for a Bible study and you wrote down several different possible ideas. Then, you noticed that all the ideas basically revolved around one core idea, namely, be careful who you follow or closely associate with.

You think to yourself, "My sticky proverb says what I believe the biblical text is saying, but it's just not that sticky." So, you decide to make it stickier by keeping the concept, but replacing the abstract truth with a symbolic word picture. You sit down at the computer, place your fingers on the keyboard, and ask your brain for a few symbolic word pictures so you can choose the best one. However, after six or seven minutes go by, you have a grand total of zero word pictures to choose from.

At that point, you do what we all do and turn to the internet for some ideas and inspiration. After a quick search on proverbs related to friends, you may find this one attributed to Benjamin Franklin, "If you lie down with dogs, you get up with fleas."

You think to yourself, "Wow! That's pretty good." You could use the proverb as is and show how it illustrates the biblical truths and application. However, you also wonder if you could keep its overall structure, but change the imagery a little to better fit your own Bible study and audience.

As you think about it, you realize your lesson is for a Friday morning Bible study primarily made up of businessmen, so you brainstorm how you might replace the imagery of dogs and waking up with fleas, with that of following dishonest bosses and waking up in an orange, prison jumpsuit.

Clearly, the stickier you make your proverb, the easier it is for everyone to remember it, but most of us don't have the time to craft a perfect proverb every time, and that's all right. Just make sure you at least craft the stickiest, concise statement you can with the time you have. As they say, "Something is better than nothing," "Half a loaf is better than none," and "Fifty percent of something is better than one hundred percent of nothing."

Let's return now to my Romans 14:13–21 example. Now that I had determined the passage's Sticky Proverb (i.e., "Before you do it, look around"), I had a better idea of how to create a focused outline that was built around this central timeless truth. Within the lesson, I explained the Sticky Proverb's meaning, demonstrated how it was the passage's timeless truth, and finally, expanded upon its application within our lives.

We talked about how others are watching everything we do and say, whether it is our kids, neighbors, friends, coworkers, or classmates. That means, before we bring up that controversial topic in class just to "liven things up," participate in a particular activity, or be involved in any other event, first look around and notice how these actions may affect others.

Now, this particular Bible study had a funny, yet convicting ending. The week after the Bible study, I was standing in the hallway talking with a few friends, and I made a comment that was fully appropriate for the two or three adults with whom I was speaking. However, I didn't notice some of the youth in the hallway who could hear our conversation, so about that time, one of the youth workers, who also overheard my comment said, "B…R…A…D," as she pointed to the youth. Then, she said with raised eyebrows, "Before you say it…look around."

Not only did she understand and remember my Bible study's Sticky Proverb, but when an applicable situation arose, she helped me apply it to my own life.

So, to summarize, first, study the passage. Second, create a Sticky Proverb. Then, third, develop the rest of the lesson.

II. Advantages of creating a Sticky Proverb
A. Helps your listeners:
1. Understand why specific information is being presented
2. Mentally organize the information

Creating this type of summary statement, or Sticky Proverb, has numerous advantages for your listeners. For example, if you write it as a short, brief principle and share it within the lesson, then it helps listeners understand why you have chosen the specific information you are sharing and how it all fits together. As they listen, they say to themselves, "Oh, I see. This information supports the point that was made at the beginning."

3. Rejoin the lesson after a distraction

Even if some get distracted during the lesson, they can start listening again and determine where you are on that journey because they know where you are headed. Yes, they missed a few of the steps along the way, but they can easily rejoin the discussion because they know the overall path you are taking and the destination you are moving toward.

4. Remember the lesson's central truth and application

And, of course, stating the lesson's central truth and application in a single memorable sentence makes it easy to remember. In fact, this may be one of the few parts of your lesson listeners remember long term. Sure, we wish they could remember the entire lesson, but at least they will remember how to apply the passage's central truth.

B. Helps the teacher:

1. Identify and clarify the lesson's teaching goal
2. Articulate the passage's primary truth and principle
3. Narrow the lesson's exact direction, angle, and focus

Developing a Sticky Proverb benefits the teacher as well. Creating a single brief catchy proverbial statement helps the teacher narrow the lesson's exact direction, angle, and focus. For example, let's say you are going to teach on love as found in 1 Corinthians 13. Fortunately, the passage contains enough wisdom that you could speak all day or all week without running out of new insights. Unfortunately, you don't have all day to teach the lesson; you have closer to thirty or forty minutes.

The real question then is, how are you going to narrow that topic down to a thirty- to forty-minute lesson? One option would be to speak as quickly as possible and to cover as many verses and principles as time allows. However, this approach doesn't usually change listeners' lives.

A better option is to look at the passage and answer the following questions:

- If I was going to make one central point, what would it be?
- Could I make the study more relevant by adding a specific angle, namely, by comparing or contrasting this central point with some aspect of life (e.g., love versus infatuation, love versus selfishness, loving the lovely versus loving the unlovely)?
- What exact area of my listeners' lives do I want to address, and what changes will they need to make?
- Which verses specifically address this central point?

4. Determine which verses need to be included or excluded

Then, use your answers to the above questions to formulate a sticky (i.e., easy to remember) proverbial-type statement that summarizes the primary truth and application you want listeners to learn from the lesson. Once you have this Sticky Proverb, you will know which aspects of the passage need to be included and which ones need to be saved for another day.

C. Prevents Ramblemation

Another huge advantage of beginning your preparation with a Sticky Proverb is it helps prevent Ramblemation. This is a lengthy discussion, so we will save it for the next chapter.

III. Sticky Proverb examples:
A. The Golden Rule

One of the greatest Sticky Proverbs ever written has been passed down from generation to generation and has even been given its own name: the Golden Rule. Here it is: "do to others what you would have them do to you" (Matthew 7:12).

Let's test some of its characteristics. Is it sticky in the sense it is easy to remember? Absolutely. Most in your class probably already know it. Is it a good summary statement? Definitely. Actually, in the same verse, Jesus says that this single Sticky Proverb sums up the entire Law and the Prophets!

Is it a nugget of wisdom that helps you apply the truth when making life decisions? Well, let's see. The Law says, "Thou shall not murder." Now, would you want someone to murder you? No, so Jesus' Sticky Proverb tells you not to murder them either. Would you want someone to commit adultery with your husband or wife; steal from you;

give false testimony against you; covet your house, your wife, or anything else that belongs to you? No, no, no, no. Therefore, you should not do that to them either. Would you want someone to cut across your lawn every day so it kills the grass? No. So the proverb tells you not to cut across their lawn either. Therefore, in a single statement, Jesus' Sticky Proverb not only summarizes the Old Testament commands but also shows us how to apply them to our lives, even in situations not specifically addressed in the Old Testament (i.e., cutting across another's lawn).

Providing a single brief memorable nugget of wisdom within your message helps listeners not only identify the passage's central truth and application but also remember it for weeks, months, years, or (as with the Golden Rule) centuries later.

B. The Trash Can

A little while ago, I was sitting in a Sunday school class behind two ladies. We were about halfway through the lesson when one of them looked at the other and said, "He's talking about the same thing we learned in that lesson about the trash can." The other lady started laughing and said, "I was just thinking the same thing." Now, what was interesting was the lesson they were referring to was taught almost two years earlier!

You may be wondering how in the world could not one but two people be listening to a lesson and then remember a different related lesson that had been taught two years earlier? The answer is simple. What they were remembering was that lesson's Visual Anchor (i.e., a large trash can being used as a visual prop) that was tied to the lesson's Sticky Proverb. Once they remembered the Visual Anchor, they remembered the lesson's Sticky Proverb: "Get Out and Stay Out." We will cover Visual Anchors in more detail in a few chapters, but for now, the point is that the truth encapsulated in that lesson's Sticky Proverb stuck with them two years later, and hopefully, it will stick with them throughout the remainder of their lives.

Within this lesson, we have seen how developing a Sticky Proverb before the creation of the lesson outline will help you determine the lesson's target, direction, emphasis, angle, focus, main points, necessary discussions, and application. In future seminars, we will build on this lesson by looking at additional methods and techniques for crafting Sticky Proverbs that enable listeners to integrate the lesson into their lives and then remember it for years to come.

3

Avoid Ramblemation

*Transform lives with lessons
focused on and centered around the Sticky Proverb*

*In your teaching
show integrity, seriousness
and soundness of speech*

— Titus 2:7–8

Chapter Outline / Notes

I. Ramblemation: a lesson's worst enemy
   A. Resist the temptation to take shortcuts

   B. Shortcuts lead to Ramblemation

II. Avoid Ramblemation by
   A. Centering your lesson around a Sticky Proverb

   B. Clearly identifying the message's timeless truth

   C. Clarifying the point and purpose of the lesson

   D. Making room for life-changing principles

III. Ramblemation examples

A. Teaching without a target

B. The <u>Jewelry-Store</u> lesson format

C. The <u>Teach-and-Tip</u> lesson format

D. The <u>Teach-and-Discuss</u> lesson format

HAVE YOU EVER BEEN IN A CONVERSATION with someone and after ten minutes you're not sure what they are saying? Even after asking a few clarifying questions and listening for another ten minutes, you still have no clue if a point exists somewhere within all those words. One topic just seems to roll into another, and another, and another. It's not that their words are incomprehensible; you just can't figure out what point they are trying to make or where the entire conversation is headed. After a while, you conclude they aren't making a point but just talking.

Even though we are careful not to speak this way in regular conversations, being aware of and preventing this form of communication is more difficult to do when teaching. It has a way of creeping into our teaching completely unnoticed. And even if it is noticed, some don't see it as a problem. After all, isn't it normal to present various topics as you work your way through a passage?

Of course, if you have gone through the previous chapter on the Sticky Proverb, you know the answer to this question is, "No!" A lesson is not the presentation of a series of related topics; rather, it is the explanation, expansion, proof, support, illustration, and application of the passage's central truth encapsulated in the Sticky Proverb.

When we begin our lesson preparation by creating a Sticky Proverb, then it helps us develop a lesson centered around a specific emphasis, angle, focus, direction, or target. It clarifies the lesson's main points, necessary discussions, potential roadblocks, and application.

---

*A lesson is not
the presentation of a series of related topics;
rather, it is the explanation, expansion,
proof, support, illustration, and
application of the primary, central truth,
namely, the Sticky Proverb.*

I. Ramblemation: a lesson's worst enemy
A. Resist the temptation to take shortcuts

So, to reiterate what we said in the last chapter, when creating a lesson, it is best to follow these steps:

1. Study the passage.
2. Create a Sticky Proverb.
3. Create a lesson outline that supports, explains, proves, and applies the Sticky Proverb to listeners' lives.

As simple as this may seem, you are going to be tempted to combine these three steps into one single step. First, you will be tempted to skip the second step and not create a Sticky Proverb. Then, you will be tempted to combine steps one and three by creating your lesson outline as you study for the lesson.

Admittedly, taking this shortcut saves time. Think about it: if you skip creating a Sticky Proverb and develop your lesson outline while studying for the lesson, then by the time you are done studying, you will almost be done with your lesson outline. Add a few illustrations and application points, and you are ready to teach.

B. Shortcuts lead to Ramblemation

Unfortunately, taking this shortcut often results in informational lessons rather than transformational ones. If the teacher does not take the time to find and develop a Sticky Proverb, then no particular central point will be explained, proved, and integrated into listeners' lives. When the lesson does not focus on a defined core truth, it often becomes an extended audible commentary that explains verse after verse and point after point.

Without a specific focus, teachers will give a lot of information and make numerous points, but they won't prove any specific overarching point. Within the thirty to forty minutes of explanation, little more than a cursory solution will be given for any particular problem. Numerous informational arrows will be shot, but instead of shooting at a specific target, they are shot in the same general direction with the hope that when they come down, they will hit some target in the listeners' lives.

Granted, when the arrows finally come down, they will hit targets here and there, but because they land all over the place, their overall impact will be minimal. No one denies the teacher has given a lot of information, but it is information without a destination ... arrows without a specific target.

The Sticky Proverb prevents
explanation without a destination,
arrows without a target.

To make it easier to refer to, I have given a name to this form of teaching where the teacher wanders from verse to verse while giving explanation along the way. I call it ramblemation.

ram·ble·ma·tion [ram-buhl-**mey**-shuhn]
noun

(1) rambling information.

(2) explanation without a destination.

(3) the act of wandering or meandering through the text giving various definitions, explanations, and background information unrelated to, or only partially related to, any particular central point or objective.

II. Avoid Ramblemation by
A. Centering your lesson around a Sticky Proverb

Once again, the best way to avoid ramblemation and create transformational lessons, rather than informational ones, is by (1) studying the passage, (2) creating a Sticky Proverb that summarizes and applies the passage's central timeless truth, and (3) developing a lesson outline that specifically supports, explains, proves, and applies the Sticky Proverb.

B. Clearly identifying the message's timeless truth

At this point, you may be thinking something like this:

> If my lesson says the same thing the biblical author says, then how can it be more informational than transformational? Surely, the biblical author's message is transformational, so if my lesson explains what he is saying, then it, too, should be transformational ... right?

And, of course, this would be correct if your audience is similar to the biblical author's audience with similar problems and struggles. However, it is unlikely your listeners still struggle with whether or not they should obey the Old Testament ceremonial laws, whether or not they should eat meat that has been offered to idols, or what is the proper way to set up the tabernacle. Instead, your listeners have a whole new set of modern issues and problems, and they want you to show them how to apply the passage's timeless truths to the contemporary problems within their lives.

Of course, many passages address problems and issues that are still relevant to our lives today, such as, marriage, parenting, truthfulness, honesty, loving one another, spiritual warfare, and many others. Even so, when you look at these passages, you still find that the biblical author is discussing these timeless truths because he is dealing with a specific issue or problem among his audience.

In other words, he's not writing because he was in the mood to write a letter that day; instead, he's writing to deal with a specific problem in the lives of his people, and that's the point! We don't teach just because it's Sunday morning and that's what we do; instead, we teach to deal with specific problems in the lives of OUR people. Teaching is not about explaining what the biblical author was saying; instead, it's figuring out and explaining how the biblical author's timeless truths fit into our lives, how they solve our specific problems, how they help our marriages, and how they help us live a godly life.

So, instead of telling them how Peter, Paul, or Moses dealt with problems among their people or problems that may not have been an issue for thousands of years now, study the passage, determine its timeless truth, create a Sticky Proverb that states that truth in a way that specifically relates to your listeners, then develop a lesson outline that specifically supports, explains, proves, and applies the Sticky Proverb to your listeners' lives.

C. Clarifying the point and purpose of the lesson

In short, the Sticky Proverb helps eliminate ramblemation by clarifying the lesson's target, direction, emphasis, angle, focus, main points, and application.

- Once you know how the passage is relevant, you know which areas of your listeners' lives need to change and how they need to change.
- Once you know how listeners' lives need to change, you know the potential objections and rationalizations your lesson has to address.
- Once you know the objections and rationalizations, you know which arrows are needed and exactly where to aim them.
- Once you know what you are trying to prove, you know what main points and supporting information is required.
- Once you know your Sticky Proverb, you know what information needs to be included to achieve your goal and what information needs to be excluded to prevent unrelated and diverting ideas.
- Once you know your Sticky Proverb, you know how to focus the lesson and prevent ramblemation.

D. Making room for life-changing principles

For example, during the study phase of your preparation, you will find a lot of interesting material that could be included in your lesson. So, how do you know what to include and what to exclude? Without a clearly defined target, or Sticky Proverb, what is often included is the most interesting material that leads to ramblemation.

On the other hand, if you start with a Sticky Proverb, it will help you identify this interesting, yet only partially related, information that needs to be cut from the lesson. Once you remove everything that doesn't directly support the Sticky Proverb, you will have room to integrate the relevant information that helps listeners understand, personally accept, and apply the passage's timeless truth to their 21st-century lives. Your goal is not to teach every thing you know, but only that which supports the point you are trying to make.

III. Ramblemation examples

In order to better understand ramblemation, let's look at four fairly common lesson formats. Initially, these appear to be sound, advantageous formats, but upon closer examination, we find that they often lead to ramblemation.

A. Teaching without a target

This first lesson format is used by teachers with various teaching styles. Some teachers focus on a particular passage and teach through it verse-by-verse, while others focus on a particular topic and provide a biblical perspective using verses scattered throughout the Bible. Either way, both sets of teachers within this first category fail to focus on a specific, defined target, intent, or aim. Their lesson neither answers a specific question burning in everyone's mind nor seeks a solution to a particular problem listeners are struggling with. Instead, their primary aim is on clearly covering the material or verses included in that week's lesson.

Of course, it is easy to understand how this happens. Teachers sit down to prepare. They read through the Sunday school quarterly or the section of Scripture for the next lesson. Then, they ask themselves a few questions such as these: "What would be the best way to present and teach this material? What background information and theological points need to be explained? Should I begin with a story? What are some good discussion-oriented questions?"

If they are not careful, their reason for presenting that particular lesson is because it was the next lesson in the quarterly. Thus, their goal is to clearly explain the material as they work their way through the passage. The end result is a lesson that is more informational than transformational.

A more effective approach is possible when the teacher's initial questions are closer to some of these: "Why should I even teach this lesson in the first place? What is in this passage that my class *must* hear? How does this passage specifically *relate to* my listeners? How can this passage help my listeners live a more godly life? What do they need to understand to be able *to integrate* this principle into their lives? What content and Scripture needs to be *included* and what needs to be *excluded* so the lesson is focused and applicable."

Then, from the answers, the teacher develops a Sticky Proverb and builds the rest of the lesson around helping listeners integrate that truth into their lives. The most effective teachers begin with a God-given quest or intent that the rest of the lesson explains, illustrates, proves, and applies to listeners' lives.

Before moving on, consider your own teaching. When you last taught, do you believe your class felt they were passionately pursuing a personally relevant issue or that they were listening to an explanation of the lesson's content?

---

*Before preparing or teaching,
clearly identify the God-given quest
the lesson will pursue.*

B. The Jewelry-Store lesson format

When your lesson isn't driving toward a specified, life-altering truth or principle, then this second format is also easy to adopt: the Jewelry Store lesson format. When using this format, the teacher invites the class up to the glass counter as the finest jewels within the passage are pulled out and displayed (or explained). Jewel after jewel, the teacher works his or her way down the counter until the end is reached and the lesson is over.

The teacher begins with the first verse and displays the shiniest spiritual gems within that verse. Then, after all of the finest truths and principles have been discussed, he moves on to the next verse. This process continues until the teacher has reached the end of the passage. At this point, he looks back down the counter, thanks God for all the jewels he has given us, and closes in prayer.

Of course, this is a fairly clear example of ramblemation. The decision of how many verses to cover and which truths to present is based on how much each truth sparkles rather than their relationship to any particular teaching goal. In other words, if it sparkles, include it; if it doesn't, move on. If it's interesting, fascinating, or deep, include it; if it's not, move on.

Without a commitment to explain, prove, and apply a specific timeless truth, it is easy to wander from verse to verse or paragraph to paragraph displaying that which sparkles the most. Unfortunately, this cursory display of the costly jewels fails to provide listeners with enough information for them to calculate if any one of the jewels is worth the investment. As a result, listeners decide to do nothing. They enjoyed looking at all the gems, so they thank the teacher for the wonderful presentation, but the jewels remain under the counter until the next time that Scripture is discussed.

You could increase this lesson's effectiveness by first finding the passage's central timeless truth. Then, instead of moving from verse to verse or paragraph to paragraph, limit yourself to the set of verses that contain this timeless truth and present all of the insights, principles, and application directly related to this truth. Next, identify the common objections and rationalizations that may hinder them from buying into this core truth. Help them overcome these hindrances with a solid biblical response and a challenge to make the necessary life changes.

Without a commitment to explain, prove,
and apply a specific timeless truth,
it is easy to wander from verse to verse
displaying that which scintillates the most.

C. The Teach-and-Tip lesson format

A third ramblemation lesson format is what I call the Teach-and-Tip format. This format is similar to the Jewelry Store format in that the teacher presents the shiniest principles for each verse. However, with this format, before moving on to the next verse, the teacher shares a few tips for how listeners can apply the various principles to their lives.

On the one hand, it is great that the teacher is including application tips within the lesson; however, as stated earlier, the tips usually have a minimal impact because they are often disjointed. The scattered tips are unable to explain, prove, illustrate, and integrate a specific central point into the listener's life. As the teacher moves from verse to verse giving various tips along the way, it is as if various arrows are being systematically shot into the air hoping they will hit something when they come down.

---

*A scattering of tips
is unable to explain, prove, illustrate, or
integrate any specific central point
into listeners' lives.*

Often, these tips tend to be "safe" and "obvious" tips that can be given quickly without much explanation or proof. They are tips listeners will easily accept or may even already agree with. But if most everyone already knows or agrees with what is about to be said, why say it? Wouldn't it be more beneficial to focus on principles listeners don't know, don't know how to apply, or aren't currently applying?

I once attended a Bible study largely consisting of mature believers. The study was on the Holy Spirit, and it followed the Teach-and-Tip format. We began in John 14:26, and after explaining how the Spirit teaches us all things, the teacher gave the following "safe" and "obvious" tip: "When we have our daily devotions, we need to depend on the Holy Spirit for insight and guidance." Then, he moved on to the next verse.

Now, with an audience largely consisting of mature believers, do you think it was obvious to those present they should depend on the Holy Spirit when reading Scripture? Do you think most of them already agreed with that tip? Probably so.

Instead of telling them what they already knew and moving on to the next verse with some more safe and obvious tips, the teacher would have been far more effective if he had stopped right there and centered the message around this one principle. This, then, would have given him time to deal with some of the common questions related to this topic, such as these:

- What exactly do I need to do to depend on the Holy Spirit when I read Scripture?
- What is the difference between studying a passage, reading a commentary on the passage, and having the Spirit teach me the passage?
- What does it signify when two different people study a passage and disagree as to what it means? Is one right and the other wrong? Are they both right or both wrong? If both of them depended on the Spirit to teach them, how could they have opposing interpretations?
- How do I know when the Holy Spirit has taught me something versus when I came up with the insight myself? If someone disagrees with my insight, how do I know if I'm right or wrong?

Clearly, numerous questions need to be answered before listeners will know how to apply this one tip to their lives. Of course, rather than providing the more difficult debatable answers to these questions, it's much easier to just say, "Depend on the Holy Spirit," and move on to the next verse. Unfortunately, these easy, generic tips have a minimal impact on listeners. To change lives, (1) study the passage, (2) create a specific Sticky Proverb based upon the passage's central timeless truth, and (3) develop a lesson outline that explicitly explains, supports, proves, and illustrates how listeners can apply the specific Sticky Proverb to their lives.

D. The Teach-and-Discuss lesson format

Before concluding, let's look at one last lesson format that often leads to ramblemation. I refer to this as the Teach-and-Discuss lesson format. This format is similar to the Teach-and-Tip format, but instead of giving a "tip" after each point, the teacher asks one or more questions related to the material and allows time for discussion.

Now, don't misunderstand what I'm saying. I am *not* discouraging the use of discussion. When used correctly, it is a highly effective teaching tool. However, *I am* discouraging discussion that wanders from topic to topic to topic rather than helping listeners understand a specific overarching biblical point. I am discouraging semi-related discussions that are loosely related to a general topic but fail to prove any particular point. I am discouraging asking a series of questions simply to create a lively small group discussion.

Of course, these wandering discussions often lead to energetic lessons full of lively dialogue as everyone shares their opinions. However, the discussions seldom change views and beliefs because they aren't working together to help listeners understand, accept, and integrate a central truth into their lives. Instead, the discussions jump from topic to topic, allowing only enough time for various individuals to share their differing views. After the topic has been kicked around a bit, but before anyone's views are changed, the lesson moves on to the next point and discussion.

―――――

Wandering disjointed discussions
lead to lively dialogue
but fail to change views, beliefs, and lives.

―――――

When preparing your next lesson, first develop the lesson's relevant Sticky Proverb, then create a lesson that explains, proves, and integrates that principle into your listeners' lives. Even though you will cover fewer topics, your teaching will have a greater overall impact. You will teach MORE by teaching LESS.

4

Captivating Introduction

*Instantly grab and hold attention by showing
listeners your lesson's application and relevance*

*How sweet are your words to my taste,
sweeter than honey to my mouth!*

— Psalm 119:103

Chapter Outline / Notes

I. **Immediately show the lesson's relevance**

A. As a restaurant creates a desire to eat, your title and introduction should create a desire to listen

B. Instead of cute, clever, or vague titles, create titles that reveal how the lesson will change their lives

II. **Focus on issues important to listeners**

A. Focus on life-changing issues

B. Avoid irrelevant, ambiguous titles and introductions

III. **First wake them, then tell them why they should stay awake**

A. Reveal the lesson's relevance in the introduction

B. But first, wake them up

C. Then, specifically tell them why they should listen

IV. Don't start with ...

    A. ... a series of semi-related questions

    B. ... a history, theology, or Greek lesson

    C. ... small talk

    D. ... an apology

    E. ... an interesting story, illustration, joke, or video clip that doesn't create a desire to listen to the remainder of the lesson

    F. ... a long, drawn-out introduction

V. Begin with why listeners should listen

WHEN KELLY AND I WERE DATING, I was in college, so money was a bit tight. Going to a nice restaurant was a treat. I remember taking Kelly to one restaurant where the chef, in his white hat and coat, stood in front of a grill with fire dancing around the sizzling steaks. As we waited for a table, I could smell all sorts of savory dishes scattered throughout the restaurant.

As our hostess led us to our table overlooking the intercoastal waterway, we passed by fresh salmon, blackened shrimp, a huge chef salad, and garlic bread. Picking a favorite was difficult, but we finally ordered. As it arrived, my mouth began to water because of the colorful, steamy, creamy, perfectly cooked vegetables and tender meat sitting in front of me. We bowed to give thanks, but I had a hard time concentrating because I kept thinking about what I should try first. It's no wonder why that chef and restaurant were able to motivate large numbers of people to take an hour out of their busy schedule and pay a chunk of money so they could come and enjoy what the chef specifically prepared for them.

I. Immediately show the lesson's relevance
A. As a restaurant creates a desire to eat, your title and introduction should create a desire to listen
Now, if you equate this dining experience with teaching God's Word, then your title and introduction should captivate your audience in the same way this first portion of our dining experience captivated us:

- We hadn't eaten yet, but we couldn't wait to start.
- We didn't know if it was going to be good, but we couldn't wait to find out!
- And even though distractions were everywhere, we easily blocked them out as we anticipated our first bite from the food sizzling in front of us.

Immediately connect listeners to the lesson by sharing its interesting, relevant, specific, life-changing truths.

Your lesson's title and introduction should create a similar response in your audience. The two should instantly connect with your listeners' lives, problems, challenges, or interests. Your title and introduction should grab everyone's attention so that they ignore all of the surrounding distractions as they anticipate what you are about to say. Your class has no idea if your lesson is going to be good, but by the end of the introduction, they can't wait to begin and find out.

B. Instead of cute, clever, or vague titles, create titles that reveal how the lesson will change their lives

Usually, the title is the first part of the lesson your listeners see or hear. Therefore, it should not be cute, clever, vague, or ambiguous so it leaves them wondering if the lesson has anything to do with them. Instead, it should be more like one of the descriptions you find for a big juicy steak in the menu. In the same way a menu describes what the customer can expect if they order the steak, the lesson title should tell listeners what they can expect if they listen to the lesson. As the menu describes what the steak is going to taste like, the lesson title should describe what the listener's life can look like and how it can be improved. In the same way the steak's title directly connects with customers' taste buds and hunger, your lesson title should directly connect with the issues in your listeners' lives.

As the sights and smells in a restaurant
create a desire to eat,
develop a title and introduction
that creates a desire to listen.

For example, the title "The Five Relationship Laws" is ambiguous and discloses little about the lesson's content. You don't know if the lesson is going to deal with relationships between friends, family members, married couples, in-laws, coworkers, neighbors, or one of the other hundred possibilities. On the other hand, if the title was "Five Ways to Affair-Proof Your Marriage," then not only do you know who the lesson will address and what aspect of the relationship it will deal with, but you also know the problem it will solve and the benefit listeners will gain from listening.

II. Focus on issues important to listeners
A. Focus on life-changing issues

Like the title, the lesson's introduction should also focus on the specific area of life that will be improved, the problem that will be solved, the mystery that will be revealed, or the question that will be answered. It should not be cute, clever, vague, or ambiguous so it leaves them wondering if the lesson has anything to do with them. Instead, it should be more like bringing them up to the grill and showing them the big juicy, sizzling steak you are about to serve. As they watch the fire jumping around the grill and smell the steak, garlic bread, and stir fry vegetables, they can't wait to begin.

B. Avoid irrelevant, ambiguous titles and introductions

This is not the time for generalities when you show them some vague mystery meat. Instead, this is the time when you show them how your lesson is specifically going to change and improve a particular area of their life. It is the time when you captivate their attention and convince them to listen.

The introduction should leave them anticipating the first bite, waiting to see if it is going to taste as wonderful as it looks and smells. It should leave them wondering if the specific area of their life can actually be as good as what they just heard in the introduction. It should leave them questioning what they need to do, know, or change so they can gain the life changes you just talked about.

By the end of the introduction, you have been successful if you can look around the room and see that everyone has scooted up to the table, has a fork in one hand and a knife in the other, and is ready for you to place the steak on their plate. However, if they are still whispering to each other, working on their shopping list, and finishing up a text message, then they are telling you they are not interested in the meal you are about to serve, and consider these other items as more important than what they believe you are about to say.

So, what happens when you don't connect your title and introduction with your listeners? What happens when the beginning of the lesson doesn't create a desire to listen? If the title is a cute or clever description that leaves listeners wondering how the lesson relates to their life or if the introduction looks like a colorless, irrelevant mystery meat, then your audience may mentally turn away from the plate you are serving and begin thinking about something else.

Once they become indifferent to what they "believe" you are serving, then, somewhere later in the lesson, you will have to work even harder to get them to mentally re-engage and start listening. It is far easier to create a desire to listen from the very beginning by showing them how the lesson will specifically benefit their life.

III. First wake them, then tell them why they should stay awake

A. Reveal the lesson's relevance in the introduction

Therefore, as the chef or teacher, we must remember that both presentation and content play a significant role in creating transformational lessons. God is responsible for providing the steak which we serve; we are responsible for presenting it in an interesting, engaging, relevant, and applicable format.

God is responsible for the substance;
we are responsible for the presentation.

Consequently, after hearing your title and introduction, either your audience will block out all the surrounding distractions in anticipation of the first bite of your message or they will mentally push the plate away, turn from the table, and begin thinking about all the surrounding distractions that appear to be more relevant to their lives. Because few will invest time and energy in something that appears irrelevant, clearly establish your lesson's relevance right up front.

Let me say that again:

Because few will invest time and energy in something that appears irrelevant, clearly establish your lesson's relevance right up front.

B. But first, wake them up

Now, you can help this whole process by waking everyone up at the very beginning of your lesson. As you stand to teach, everyone is thinking about various issues. Some are thinking about last nights events, others are thinking about what they need to do on the way home from church, and still others are thinking about Sally's prayer request or anything else that was said just before you stood up.

So, at the very beginning of your introduction, you need to grab everyone's attention so you can successfully show them the juicy steak you are about to serve. For example, within the first thirty seconds, do something out of the ordinary that causes everyone to look up and say, "Wait, what's going on? Why is he doing that?" You can do something as simple as starting your lesson from a different location in the room, placing in front of them a large sealed bag containing a prop, or any other uncommon action that causes them to momentarily stop what they are doing, look up, and listen to your first sentence or two.

C. Then, specifically tell them why they should listen

Of course, what you say within these first two sentences is critical and needs to create a desire to listen to the remainder of the introduction. Then, throughout the introduction, share your Sticky Proverb, the text for the day, the convincing reasons why they must continue to listen, and how it will impact a specific area of their life.

First wake them up, then tell them why they should stay awake. First break through all the distractions, then help them ignore the distractions by telling them one or more of the following:

- the area of life that will be improved
- the need that will be met
- the problem that will be solved
- the issue that will be resolved
- the secret that will be revealed
- the puzzle that will be unraveled
- the threat that will be alleviated
- the critical information that will be disclosed
- the mystery that will be unwrapped
- the question that will be answered

Of course, sometimes listeners incorrectly assume they have already met the need, solved the problem, discovered the secret, answered the question, alleviated the threat, and so forth. In these cases, you will be unable to grab and hold their attention by telling them the lesson is going to focus on what they "believe" they already know or have already figured out.

In other words, your introduction will fail if you tell them you are about to solve a problem they do not believe they have or if you tell them you're about to alleviate a threat they don't believe exists. For these topics, your introduction has to first help them realize the error of their previously held view, answer, or solution. Then, and only then, will you have their full attention. In short, help them realize the problem still needs to be solved or the threat is still looming over some area of their life. Of course, if they actually *do* know the answer or solution, you don't want to teach on that topic anyway ... right?

For example, let's say the next lesson in the Sunday school curriculum is on parenting children, but your class consist of seniors. In their minds, their parenting years are largely over. In fact, their children are in their 30s and 40s and have small children of their own.

So, should you teach on parenting anyway? Well, probably not in the same way it is presented in the curriculum. You could either skip that lesson or adjust it a bit and talk about how to be a godly grandparent. If your class spends any time at all with the grand kids, many relevant issues can be taught such as how do you discipline grand kids, how do you share the gospel with young children, how do you share a biblical perspective on issues they are struggling with, etc. No matter who you are teaching and what the subject is, within the introduction, make sure to reveal how the lesson directly connects with a specific area in your listeners' life.

So, by the end of the introduction, you need to make sure you have captured their attention by showing them how the lesson is about to improve a specific area of their life.

First, tell them why they should listen, then they will be ready to hear what the Bible says about the topic that now has their interest.

In other words, within the first few minutes, make sure they have entered the restaurant, they have seen and smelled much that looks tasty, and that you have placed in front of them a plate sizzling with a colorful, steamy, creamy, interesting, relevant, specific, personalized, clear and simple, life-changing improvement. Make sure they know that what you are about to say is far more relevant to their life than anything else they may consider thinking about. That is the goal of the title and introduction.

IV. Don't start with ...

Of course, most teachers attempt to serve an introductory plate full of sizzling, attention-getting, life-changing truths. However, this does not always happen because they are uncertain how to consistently prepare this type of dish. As a result, they end up choosing one of the less desirable standby dishes. Let's next take a look at some of these less desirable introductory dishes that listeners perceive as irrelevant and are therefore best avoided.

A. ... a series of semi-related questions

One introductory dish you want to avoid includes beginning with a series of superficial questions that lead to a shallow discussion. Of course, no one intends to begin with a series of superficial questions, but rather, questions that lead to an exciting discussion. However, the exciting discussion doesn't always happen for a few different reasons.

When you first begin, listeners are unsure of the lesson's content or direction. Therefore, any initial set of questions often receive vague or general answers because it is unclear what answer you are looking for. And even when they know the point or topic of the lesson, because the questions come before any teaching, listeners often don't have enough information to develop solid answers.

As a result, the answers and discussions tend to be shallow, filled with a lot of "here's-what-I-think" opinions. Of course, for those who love to share their opinion, this is great, but for others, they lose interest and begin thinking about issues they believe are "more relevant" to their lives, like what they are going to eat for lunch. It is often more profitable to ask discussion-oriented questions after you have taught for a while and given listeners enough information to develop views and opinions.

I'm not saying you should never start a lesson with a question. Sometimes, the right question at the right time can have a significant impact on one's thinking. Other times, questions can be used to achieve specific teaching goals, such as creating a Knowledge Gap in the listener's mind (a topic we will cover in a future seminar). You may even begin with a single question just to wake everyone up and generate interest in the lesson's topic, but these types of questions are different from those whose primary purpose is to generate a discussion that lasts longer than a few minutes.

B. ... a history, theology, or Greek lesson

A second introductory dish best avoided includes beginning your lesson with detailed academic-type information. For example, some teachers may begin with the historical background of the passage, the theological view supported by the text, a Greek word study, or some other array of information. Even though this may need to be included later in the lesson (even possibly the first thing you cover after the introduction), if you give it before listeners understand why it matters or how it is going to change their lives, those uninterested in that specific type of information may lose interest and begin thinking about something else.

Within the introduction, you will certainly share the topic and biblical passage the lesson centers around, but that is far different than beginning with a theological overview of the passage. First, tell them *why* they should listen, then tell them *what* the Bible says about it. Once they understand why it matters, they will be ready and waiting for what it means, what theological implications are within the passage, what needs to change in their life, and more.

C. ... small talk

Third, don't begin your lesson with small talk, such as the following:

> Good morning. I hope everyone is awake. If you
> need to refill your coffee cup, feel free to do so.

Mike, thanks for making the announcements this morning. If you have your Bible, please open it to Ephesians 6:4. Oh, and let's thank Mary for bringing the snack today. That was delicious. Anyway, today we are going to look at what Paul has to say about fathers exasperating their children. Has anyone found the verse yet? Would someone like to read that for us? While you are finding the passage, let me make one other quick announcement…

I realize beginning with small talk is a fairly common way to begin a lesson, but it is a habit worth breaking. Once the lesson begins, the teacher's first job is to capture everyone's attention so they stop thinking about everything going on in their life along with all of the announcements and prayer requests that have just been given. However, if their introduction includes small talk and additional announcements, then it simply interjects new distractions and gives listeners even more to think about. Instead of redirecting their attention toward the lesson, their small talk distracts listeners even further.

D. … an interesting story, illustration, or video clip that fails to create a desire to listen to the remainder of the lesson

Another type of introduction that is best avoided is one that incorporates a story, illustration, or video clip simply because it is related to the lesson and is interesting to the listeners. No matter how interesting the material is, if it does not convince the audience to listen to the remainder of the lesson, then your introduction has failed to do its job.

Remember, the primary goal of the introduction is not to entertain your audience. It is not to introduce the topic, passage, or lesson. Rather, the primary goal of the introduction is to captivate your audience's attention and create within them a tremendous desire to listen to the lesson. If your introduction motivates everyone to stop eating their donuts and drinking their coffee in anticipation of what will be said next, then it has done its job and you are ready to move on. First, tell them *why* they should listen, then they will be ready to hear *what* the Bible says about the topic that now has their interest.

The goal of the introduction is NOT
to introduce the lesson, but
to create a huge desire
to listen to the lesson.

E. ... an apology

Fifth, don't start with an apology for why the lesson is going to be substandard or lacking. Here are a few common apologies:

- This is my first time teaching, so bear with me.
- It sure is a lot different standing up here than sitting

out there. I hope I don't forget everything I was going to say.

- Boy, I haven't taught for a while, and I'm a little nervous, so I'm hoping for the best.
- I'm not feeling well today, but I'll do my best.
- Today's topic is difficult to understand, so I may need your help and comments.
- I didn't have as much time as I wanted to prepare this week's lesson, so this may be shorter than normal.

If you begin with an apology, you might as well say, "Hey, today's lesson is going to be a bit boring, so you might as well tune out now." Rather than making excuses for what has been excluded, trust God to change lives through what will be included.

F. ... a long, drawn-out introduction

Last, avoid beginning with long, drawn-out stories, illustrations, class participation exercises, discussions, dramas, or other similar activities. Such introductions often leave listeners wondering if the lesson has started, and if it has, what in the world is it about. When possible, try to grab their attention within the first thirty seconds by beginning with something out of the ordinary; then within the next few minutes, reveal how the lesson is going to be relevant to their lives. If after five or ten minutes, you are still in the introduction and haven't specifically informed them of the lesson's topic or relevance, then you may have already lost many of them.

V. Begin with why listeners should listen

The point is this: skip the apologies, small talk, historical backgrounds, and other similar introductions, and begin with the very reason your listeners should listen. Instead of starting with an introduction that may or may not interest them, tell them *why* the lesson matters, *how* it will benefit them, and *what* is at stake if they fail to listen.

Don't begin with anything that may cause some to drift off and think about anything other than your lesson. Be careful not to present information that is interesting to you but not everyone else. The goal of the introduction is certainly to focus everyone on the text, but more importantly, it is to create a desire to *listen*! Once they are listening, you have the rest of the lesson to say everything else.

The goal of the introduction is to CREATE A DESIRE TO LISTEN; then you have the rest of the lesson to say everything else.

For example, let's say you are preparing a lesson for a married adult class. Since you are the chef, you can create an introduction that gets right to the point like this:

Example 1:

Albert Einstein said, "Women marry men hoping they will change. Men marry women hoping they will not." What, then, happens to our marriage when he never changes and she changes drastically? How do we deal with our disappointments? How do we love someone who doesn't become the person we thought we were marrying? I'm not asking how do we put up with them or how do we get along with them; I'm asking, how do we sincerely love them?

Example 2:

Do you ever wonder why our kids sometimes get mad at us for no apparent reason? Have you ever tried to be interested in their lives and asked something like, "How did your date go last night?" or "How did your test go last week?" and they blow up for no apparent reason? Or maybe you attempt to help them with homework or a project, and the harder you try, the more irritated they become. These responses leave us wondering, "What just happened? What did I do that caused them to get so irritated?" Well, I believe I've figured out at least one thing we do to cause this kind of response in our kids. Actually, Paul talks about it in Ephesians 6:4.

Notice how both of these introductions begin by promising a benefit, namely, by promising to solve an actual heartfelt problem. They don't start with an apology, small talk, information, reading the text for that day, a historical background of marriage in the New Testament, or a series of questions about what's wrong with parenting in America. Instead, they immediately touch a sensitive nerve in many of the listeners' lives and promise a solution to the problem.

And even if some of your listeners have dodged these issues so far, they will want to know how to prevent them from cropping up in the future. Either way, by the end of the introduction, most of those within the married adult class are probably engaged and waiting to see if your lesson is going to deliver what the introduction sounds like it is promising.

For many, including application in the introduction feels a little backward because they usually save it for the conclusion. They teach through the entire lesson, then near the end, they say something like, "OK, let's now see how this applies to our lives." What I am suggesting is to switch this order and share the lesson's relevance and application at the beginning so everyone has a huge reason to listen to the rest of your message. You may have to wait until the end of the lesson to explain the exact steps needed to apply the principles, but the introduction can at least share what areas of their life will be altered by the lesson.

Within this chapter, we have looked at the importance of creating titles and introductions that, first, immediately engage your audience, and then second, give them life-changing reasons to listen to the remainder of the lesson. As you prepare your next lesson, make sure the title and introduction connect your listeners to your lesson by revealing the interesting, relevant, specific, personalized, life-changing truths you are about to share. Rather than beginning with a series of shallow questions, a history lesson, small talk, or an apology, introduce the lesson by promising to tackle a problem, reveal a mystery, tell a secret, answer a question, meet a need, solve a puzzle, alleviate an issue, disclose critical information, or improve an area of their lives.

5

The Visual Anchor

*Create a lesson listeners will remember
for five or ten years ... maybe a lifetime*

*My son, do not forget my teaching,
but keep my commands in your heart,*

— Proverbs 3:1

Chapter Outline / Notes

I. Connect your Sticky Proverb to a Visual Anchor

II. For truths that need to be remembered, give a picture; for everything else, abstract truths work just fine

III. Characteristics of a good Visual Anchor
  A. Concrete

  B. Previously known

  C. Ridiculous, crazy, impossible, illogical, absurd

  D. Disproportionate

  E. Exaggerated

  F. Animated

IV. A few Visual-Anchor teaching tips

  A. Know your audience

  B. Don't let your comfort zone limit your presentation

V. The stepping-stone example

*I*N AN EARLIER CHAPTER, I TOLD YOU ABOUT a time when two ladies were sitting in front of me during a Sunday school lesson. About halfway through the lesson, one of the ladies turned to the other and said, "He's talking about the same thing we learned in the *trash can lesson*." The other lady started laughing and said, "I was just thinking the same thing."

These two ladies had heard thousands of lessons over the course of their lives, so what caused both of them, at the same time, to remember a lesson they had heard over two years ago? What caused them to realize the previous lesson directly applied to their current situation? If you're wanting to teach lessons that have the same lifelong impact on your listeners, these are questions worth pondering and finding the answers to.

Another time, I overheard two classmates chatting several days after hearing a lesson on making the most of the opportunities God gives us. About halfway through the conversation, one man said to the other, "Tick, Tick, Tick," and the other smiled and said, "Yeah, I know. I've been thinking about that lesson all week." Think about that: three words conveyed the truth of the lesson.

Again, what enabled these two men not only to remember that lesson's truth but also to apply it to their current situation? The answer to this question is easily one of the most significant teaching principles I have discovered over the years, so let's look at it next.

I. Connect your Sticky Proverb to a Visual Anchor

The primary answer to the above questions revolves around the lesson's "Visual Anchor." A Visual Anchor helps listeners remember the truths in a lesson by connecting or linking them to a visual concrete image, object, story, illustration, analogy, example, metaphor, testimony, or real-life situation. In the two examples above, the truths in the lesson were associated with a trash can in the first example and a ticking clock in the second example. In both cases, it was the lesson's Visual Anchor that enabled them to remember the truth connected to it.

Visual concrete images are like mental anchors that lodge in listeners' memories and remain there for weeks, months, years, or even a lifetime. Consequently, if you tie your lesson's Sticky Proverb and main truths to a Visual Anchor, they too can be remembered for a lifetime. The better you design the anchor, the longer it will stick in listeners' memories.

Of course, sometimes it is difficult to relate the Visual Anchor to your Sticky Proverb along with each of the main points. Actually, this is often pretty tough to do. So, in this case, you should connect it to your sticky proverb since the sticky proverb sums up the entire lesson's truth and application in a single, concise statement. Actually, the Visual Anchor should always relate directly to the Sticky Proverb. If you can also relate it to some or all of the main points, that is simply an added bonus.

II. For truths that need to be remembered, give a picture; for everything else, abstract truths work just fine

If you want listeners to remember your lesson, give them a picture; if you don't mind them forgetting, give them an abstract truth. For example, in the last chapter, we looked at the goal and purpose of a lesson's title and introduction. Of course, I stated these truths abstractly, but notice how I also visually tied them to the concrete sights, sounds, and smells of walking into a restaurant. I tied the goal and purpose of a lesson's title and introduction to your desire to eat the colorful, steamy, creamy, perfectly cooked vegetables and steak served in your favorite restaurant.

---

*If you want listeners to remember your lesson,
give them a picture;
if you don't mind them forgetting,
abstract truths work just fine.*

Similarly, this is why I gave this teaching principle the name "Visual Anchor." I could have chosen many other names, but I chose this particular name because the function of a real-life anchor is similar to the function of the abstract principle I am tying it to. Thus, by tying the two together, you can now visualize the abstract principle and remember it far longer than if I had stated it only abstractly.

For example, the teaching principle could have been stated abstractly like this:

Within each lesson, include a perceptible domi-
nate image that enables listeners to visualize the
lesson's primary truth.

Now, even though this clearly defines the principle,
most find it far easier to understand and remember a
visual concrete definition or explanation, such as this:

For each lesson, tie one end of a rope to your lesson's Sticky Proverb, then tie the other end to a
Visual Anchor, i.e., a visual concrete image, object,
story, illustration, analogy, example, metaphor,
testimony, or real-life situation. Then, when you
share this concrete image, it will lodge and stick in
your listener's memory. When listeners remember
the Visual Anchor, they will remember the Sticky
Proverb tied to it.

For whatever reason, it is easier for us to understand
and remember what we can see, hear, touch, smell, or
taste than what is stated as an abstract truth. If you went
through the lessons in the first book in this series, you will
remember how I used an hourglass as a Visual Anchor
to convey how little sand (e.g., time) God has given us
to accomplish all we hope to accomplish within our lifetime. For most of us, saying, "You don't have a lot of time
left," doesn't have the same impact as watching our sand
trickle away. Then, when we see how much of the sand
that used to fill the top portion of our hourglass is now
settled in the bottom portion, it has a way of making our
finite life span a reality.

The important point to remember here is to ensure your Visual Anchor is primarily attached to your Sticky Proverb, and secondarily, to other main points. Too many times, Visual Anchors are included within the lesson (which is great); however, they are attached to small, incidental side points. Fortunately, they still help listeners remember part of the lesson; unfortunately, that part just happens to be one of the less-relevant sub-points.

Admittedly, it's easy to understand how this happens. While preparing the lesson, the teacher comes across something that would make a great Visual Anchor. The only problem is it scarcely relates to the lesson or to just one of the minor points. Nonetheless, it is such a great Anchor, the teacher uses it anyway. Subsequently, what ends up sticking in the listener's memory is one of the less-significant side points rather than the main point.

In short, make sure your Visual Anchor is tied directly to your Sticky Proverb, not a side point, sub-point, or other supporting information.

III. Characteristics of a good Visual Anchor

When choosing or creating a Visual Anchor, realize that some are far more effective than others. Less effective Visual Anchors may only be remembered for a day or two, whereas more effective ones can be remembered for a lifetime. Fortunately, learning to create highly effective Visual Anchors is not difficult. The first step includes incorporating some of the following memory-enhancing characteristics into the object or image you will be using.

A. Concrete

One of the most important ways to make your Visual Anchor effective is to make it concrete as opposed to abstract. Sometimes your Visual Anchor may be a physical object listeners can see, touch, hear, smell, or taste. Other times, it may be a mental image they sense only in their imagination. Either way, make sure it is concrete since concrete images are remembered far longer than facts, figures, theories, principles, and other abstract information.

B. Previously known

One reason a Visual Anchor aids the memory is because it ties, connects, or links the new information in your lesson to concrete objects already familiar to your listeners. As listeners visualize the familiar concrete object (i.e., the Visual Anchor), it reminds them of the new information presented in the lesson.

Most of the time, for your Visual Anchor, you will naturally pick objects and images already familiar to your class, but every now and then, you may be tempted to choose an image specific to a hobby or area of expertise. While the object may be familiar to you, it will be unfamiliar to others. In this case, learners first have to learn about the new, unfamiliar object before they will be able to connect it to the new information within the lesson. Consequently, the link between the memory, the unfamiliar Visual Anchor, and the lesson's new information is weakened.

Let me give you an example. Let's say you are a sports fanatic and your lesson centers around a character trait exemplified by a particular player, so you decide to use the player as a visual anchor. However, for those in your class who do not watch sports, they have no idea who you are talking about. For you, the player is a concrete object who exemplifies the point your lesson is making, but for these non-sports listeners, your Visual Anchor is not a concrete person, but rather an abstract, faceless name. So, make sure to use concrete objects previously known to everyone present.

C. Ridiculous, crazy, impossible, illogical, absurd

One principle that has been known for thousands of years now is that God made it easier for us to remember ridiculous, crazy, wild, impossible, illogical, unusual, unbelievable, or absurd images much more readily than images that are plain, normal, logical, sensible, obvious, and common.

One of the oldest surviving Latin books on rhetoric, which is still used today as a textbook for rhetoric and persuasion, is *Rhetorica ad Herennium* (dating from the 90s BC). It stated this principle over 2000 years ago:

Now nature herself teaches us what we should do. When we see in everyday life things that are petty, ordinary, and banal, we generally fail to remember them, because the mind is not being stirred by anything novel or marvellous. But if we see or hear something exceptionally base, dishonourable, extraordinary, great, unbelievable, or laughable, that we are likely to remember a long time. Accordingly, things immediate to our eye or

ear we commonly forget; incidents of our child-
hood we often remember best. Nor could this be
so for any other reason than that ordinary things
easily slip from the memory while the striking
and novel stay longer in mind.[1]

For example, in the chapter on the Sticky Proverb, we
looked at a lesson where I used a large trash can to illustrate the truths within the lesson (see page 40). For
most, this was anything but normal.

Often, when preparing a lesson, I look for real-life
problems or situations that directly relate to the lesson's
truths, but which most people don't know how to solve.
In short, I look for an "impossible" situation that doesn't
appear to have a solution. Then, if possible, I tie this problem to my Visual Anchor and provide the solution within
the lesson.

Other times, some biblical passages look like they
are illogical, absurd, or irrelevant for our contemporary culture. Of course, I am quick to point this out at
the beginning of the lesson and incorporate it into my
Visual Anchor so that by the end of the lesson, the illogical becomes logical, the absurd becomes clear, and the
irrelevant becomes relevant.

D. Disproportionate

When creating a Visual Anchor, stretch the size (huge or
tiny); the speed at which it works; how much it weighs;

---

1 *Rhetorica ad Herennium*, trans. Harry Caplan (Cambridge, MA:
Harvard University Press, 1954), III xxii.

its height, color, smell, or any other aspect that can be distorted. When you pick a physical object, find the biggest or smallest example of it, the brightest, the smelliest, the loudest, the most obnoxious, the rudest, the tallest or shortest, etc. Just remember, the more out of proportion your object is from the norm, the more it will stick in the listener's memory.

For example, for the trash can lesson, when choosing a trash can for my Visual Anchor, I didn't pick one of the smaller bedroom waste baskets, nor the larger one from the kitchen. No, I chose an outside trash can that is four feet tall and two to three feet wide. In order to get it to church, I had to take the back seat out of our van so it would fit. Plus, do you think I washed it out before bringing it? Not a chance!

E. Exaggerated

When possible, exaggerate some aspect of the Visual Anchor. For example, with the trash can lesson, if I was relating the trash in the can to the sin in our lives, then I wouldn't have just a little bit of trash in the can; it would be overflowing.

I would begin with the trash can in the back of the room and push it toward the front as I began the lesson. To exaggerate this even more, before class, I could set up the chairs a little differently so I could take a longer route, pushing the trash can between a few of the rows. And of course, trash would be dropping out with every step. By the time I made it to the front, trash would be scattered all throughout the room.

If one of my points related to how our sin affects others, well, there you have it, I would point to my trash (or sin) scattered all throughout the room and talk about how everyone has to sit in the middle of my mess.

If another point related to how we see ourselves as relatively "good" people, I would point to the amount of trash in the can and talk about what we are really like.

F. Animated

Also, try to incorporate action since it makes the event more memorable and ensures everyone will stay awake throughout the entire lesson. If they were asleep before, they will wake up when something unusual happens with a lot of movement.

In the trash can lesson, at one point, I talked about how God delivers us from sin, and if we will allow him, he will remove it from our lives. So, to add action to the lesson, what do you think I did? You got it. I began tossing trash out of the can. What do you think? Did I gently put it on the ground in front of me? No, the trash left the can with a little action behind it.

To strengthen the connection between the biblical principle and the action, you could do something like this. Pick up an empty two-liter bottle and say, "Even though there are certain sins in our lives that we have tried for years to get rid of, can God still deliver us from them? You bet he can." And then toss the bottle out.

As we pick up the next piece of trash, we say, "Maybe we struggle with gossip. God can and will deliver us from that. And toss that piece out as well.

Picking up the next piece, "What about lust? Can and will God deliver us from that if we allow him to? You bet he can." And out it goes.

Repeat this five or six more times, and they will not forget that point for a long, long time. Afterward, clearly explain the lesson's scriptural principles, challenge them to make the changes, and watch your teaching transform lives.

IV. A few Visual-Anchor teaching tips
A. Know your audience

Now, let me give a few quick teaching tips before moving on to the stepping-stone example. First, when choosing your Visual Anchor, you have to know your audience to know what is appropriate. For example, if you teach children and begin tossing trash, they'd gladly join in the fun, and you'd quickly lose control of the class. If you teach youth, they'd love it and would be hanging on to your every word. If you teach seniors, they may toss you in the trash can and roll you and your example out into the hallway.

B. Don't let your comfort zone limit your presentation

Second, don't let your comfort zone dictate your presentation. After hearing the above example, some of you may be thinking, "Yeah, that's a great idea, but that's just not me ... I would feel *uncomfortable* being that animated."

It is true we are all different, with diverse teaching styles and personalities, but we should not allow these to prevent us from trying new techniques and developing a more effective teaching style. If a circle represents our teaching style, then most of us probably spend the majority of our teaching time somewhere within that circle. However, I would encourage you to increase your effectiveness by constantly expanding your circle's radius and teaching outside of this comfort zone.

Effective teachers constantly expand the circle representing their teaching style and teach outside of that circle on a regular basis.

For I did not speak of my own accord, but the Father who sent me commanded me *what to say* and *how to say it.*

—John 12:49

V. The stepping-stone example

Let's look at one final Visual Anchor example by analyzing a lesson where I used stepping-stones to represent the brevity of life. The interesting thing about this lesson is, even though I was the one who taught it, I can't remember its title or main points. Nevertheless, I can tell you what the lesson was about because I can remember its Visual Anchor.

My guess is the same is true for many of the others who were present. As a matter of fact, one of those present was a pastor. Several months after the lesson, he was preparing a sermon on a similar topic, and the stepping-stone Visual Anchor caused him to remember the lesson. Since the two messages had a similar topic, he decided to share the stepping-stone Visual Anchor in his sermon.

To better understand how to create and incorporate a Visual Anchor into a lesson, let's look at the stepping-stone lesson. The text for the study was James 4:14–15.

> Yet you do not know what your life will be like tomorrow. You are just a vapor that appears for a little while and then vanishes away. Instead, you ought to say, "If the Lord wills, we will live and also do this or that."

The first thing I noticed was James had already included the visual element of vapor appearing and vanishing, so I considered making that my own Visual Anchor. However, since this was a familiar passage to my audience, I felt they may think, "Yeah, yeah, I've already heard this before," and ignore the rest of the lesson, assuming they already knew what it was going to be about. As a result, I decided to create a fresh, new Visual Anchor to illustrate James's point.

I next considered my audience and realized it included individuals from a wide age span. This meant some of the younger ones probably felt they had enough time to pursue both their own interests as well as the things of God. Of course, this false perspective of time is why James gave the warning in the first place. James's point is life is too short to leave God out of even one portion of it. Life is like a vapor. It appears for a short time. Then it vanishes.

At that point, the big question was, "What should I use for my Visual Anchor? How can I help my audience visualize this truth in a way that will potentially lock it into their memories for the rest of their lives?" Here's what I came up with. I placed eight stepping-stones on the ground labeled Birth-9, 10–19, 20–29, 30–39, and so forth with the last one labeled 70–79+.

I began by discussing how we all start out on the first step. We then have the opportunity to take up to seven additional steps before our lives are over. I then asked an eight-year-old to come up and help me by standing on the first stepping-stone. As she took her place, I continued:

> We all spend our first few years learning the fundamentals of life. We learn to crawl, walk, and talk. Our first four words are Mama, Dada, No, and *mine*, and with that, we discover two of the primary forces that shape our lives: our parents and our sin nature.

Next, I asked a teenager to come up and stand on the second step as I continued:

> If you are a teen, look at the steps in front of you. Notice how you have six more. This means you have a few more than the rest of us, but first, James tells us you are not guaranteed of making it even to the next step, and second, as those in front of you will tell you, each step goes by quickly.
>
> Your teen years are a wonderful phase of life when you will build numerous lifelong friends and

have the opportunity to witness to them. However, even though it may feel as if this phase is taking forever to pass, before you know it, you will graduate and move on to college or the working world. You are going to discover how little time you actually have to accomplish everything God wants you to accomplish during high school. Once these years come to a close, so will the particular opportunities God has given you during this period.

Then, I talked about the importance of developing a spiritual foundation that provides the wisdom, morals, and values that lead to godly lifelong decisions. I also listed some of the opportunities youth have only during their high school years and other opportunities specific to individual years (e.g., sophomore, junior, senior).

I then addressed those on the next several steps.

For those who have successfully stepped into your twenties, you may still be thinking you have a lot of time, but notice only five steps remain. Unlike your previous step, this one will feel as if it is passing more quickly since you will be busy with activities such as finishing college, getting married, starting your first job, filing your first tax return, buying your first home, having kids, advancing in your job, raising young children, maintaining a close marriage, and more. In fact, it can be so busy, many leave God out of most of it, not to mention missing the numerous spiritual opportunities available only during this step.

For example, children go through their developmental years just once. When they are young, they are an open sponge and will learn from you all day long; however, once they hit their teen years, this openness to your thoughts and opinions seems to come to a standstill. After all, what can you possibly know ... you're their parent. Consequently, if you allow "other" activities to limit the time you spend with your kids during their first few years, this teaching opportunity will come and go, never to return. It will be a missed opportunity. Like a hummingbird, it hovers for a moment, then it is gone.

For those in your thirties, congratulations! You are getting your head together just in time for your body to start falling apart. You have begun to realize much of what your dad said was right just in time for your kids to start thinking most of what you say is wrong. You are becoming aware that the average life span is around 78 years of age, which means by the end of this step, your life will be halfway over. If you haven't already begun your mid-life crisis, you need to get on with it.

Of course, we all assume we are the exception to the rule and will live well beyond the average life span, but then again, this is the very thinking James warns us about: always assuming we have more time than we really have [James 4:15]. More than likely, you're going to be just like the rest of us and your life is now almost half over. If you're pursuing your own dreams, while thinking you have all kinds of time to pursue the things of God, I hope you're realizing the fallacy of this belief. What you are pursuing right now is what your life will consist of.

For those in your forties, you are going to realize for the first time the volume knob also turns to the left. Of course, you'll have to put your glasses on to figure out which knob to turn. Within this step, some of you will watch your little chicks fly off leaving the nest empty and quiet. We all assume we have tomorrow or next week to build into our kids everything they need for life, but in reality, it's more like two steps. Along the same lines, we assume we have forever to complete all the goals and dreams we had in our younger years, but now we begin to realize many of us will be grandparents in the next step and retiring in one and a half steps!

Two steps to grow yourself up. Two steps to grow your kids up. One and a half steps to help them get established while you prepare for retirement, then you retire. That's it. That's all you get. You can't start over, and you can't undo that which has been done.

———

Of course, I don't need to go through all the steps, and the lesson doesn't have to include just going through each of the steps, but you get the idea. As everyone mentally stood there on their step, they could look back and see what opportunities they had already missed. Then, they could look down and see everything they should be doing right now. Last, they could look forward and see how few steps they have left to accomplish everything else they want to do during this lifetime. By the end of the lesson, everyone had visually experienced the truth of James 4:14–15, and I hope it was an experience they still remember today thanks to the help of the Visual Anchor.

6

Here's-How Teaching

Teach lessons listeners can apply

All Scripture is God-breathed and is useful for teaching, rebuking, correcting and training in righteousness, so that the man of God may be thoroughly equipped for every good work.

— 2 Timothy 3:16–17

Chapter Outline / Notes

I. **Include explanation and application**
   A. Explain the original meaning of the biblical text

   B. Clarify the timeless truth

   C. Apply it to today's culture

II. **Give explicit application, not ambiguous You-Should exhortations**

III. **Become a Here's-How teacher, not a "You-Should" teacher**
   A. You-Should teachers give a quick, vague application tip, then move on

   B. Here's-How teachers explain the timeless truth and demonstrate how it can be applied

C. You-Should teachers may depend on guilt

D. Here's-How teachers depend on the Holy Spirit

IV. Correct, rebuke, and encourage with "great patience and careful instruction"

V. Prove that what you are saying is the same thing the Bible is saying
A. Prove that your application is biblically oriented

B. Proof-texting and topical teaching often lack proof

VI. Exclude topics not directly related to your Sticky Proverb
A. Omit semi-related information even if it is interesting, educational, or funny

B. Include that which directly supports the Sticky Proverb

*I*N OUR STUDY UP TO THIS POINT, we have looked at the first four teaching elements of a transformational lesson: the **Sticky Proverb** that succinctly states the lesson's primary truth and application in a memorable, applicable way; **Ramblemation** that is the result of a lesson not centered around a Sticky Proverb; the **Captivating Introduction** where you instantly grab and hold attention by connecting listeners to the lesson's application and relevance; and the **Visual Anchor** that helps listeners remember the message by connecting the Sticky Proverb and main points to a visual concrete image, object, story, illustration, or real-life situation.

In the last three chapters, we will look at three additional elements: **Here's-How Teaching**, **Removing Roadblocks**, and the **Conclusion Challenge**.

I. Include explanation and application

If our goal is to create doers of the Word and not hearers only (James 1:23–25), then we need to incorporate the following principles into the Bible study portion of each lesson.

A. Explain the original meaning of the biblical text
B. Clarify the timeless truth
C. Apply it to today's culture

For every lesson, first explain *what* the biblical text says, then demonstrate *how* it can be applied in today's culture. You need both parts: explanation and application. It is not enough to simply interpret the biblical text and explain what it meant to the original audience; you also need to show how we can integrate the truths into our 21st-century lives.

So, in addition to explaining the biblical text that addresses a particular situation within biblical history, explain how its timeless truths apply to our lives today. Explanation without application often ends in frustration because listeners realize something in their lives should change as a result of what they just heard–they're just not sure what it is.

II. Give explicit application, not ambiguous You-Should exhortations

When discussing application, it is important to make a clear distinction between *explicit application* and *You-Should exhortations*. Application clearly explains how we can obey biblical principles even if it means providing a step-by-step process every now and then. You-Should exhortations, on the other hand, don't tell listeners how to apply the truths but simply that they *should, ought to,* or *need to* apply the truths. These exhortations sound more like this:

- *You should* love your neighbor as yourself.
- *You need to* live a godly life.
- *You ought to* be a witness to your neighbors.
- *We should* remove all idols from our lives.
- *We need to* discover our spiritual gifts and use them.

And on and on it goes. Even though these statements may look like application, they are not. Listeners want you to tell them *how* they can pray without ceasing, not that they *need to* pray without ceasing. They want to know *how* they can be filled with the Spirit, not that they *should* be filled with the Spirit. Most individuals already know what they should be doing; what they want is for you to tell them *how* they can actually do it.

When you're teaching, a mental alarm should go off every time you hear yourself say, "we should," "you ought to," or "we need to" do this or that. Let this alarm remind you to follow up that You-Should exhortation with a "Here's How" application. Most of us would probably be surprised at how often we say, "you should do this," without ever following it up with "and here's how." It's not uncommon to hear teachers get on a role and rattle off five or ten You-Should exhortations without giving a single "and here's how" application.

One way to overcome "You Should" teaching is to record your lesson. This allows you to go back and make sure the majority of your You-Should exhortations were followed up with "and here's how you can do that" application. Recording yourself also allows you to discover other areas needing improvement. Often, just becoming aware of a particular habit or practice is all that is needed to make the change.

You can instantly double, triple, or even quadruple your effectiveness as a teacher, if you can learn to apply this one principle.

III. Become a Here's-How teacher, not a "You-Should" teacher

Now, I'll be the first to tell you that being a Here's-How teacher, who gives explicit application, is far more difficult than being a You-Should teacher. Look at the following examples and note how much easier it is to give the "You Should" exhortations than to figure out and provide the additional Here's-How application.

Easy: *"You should* love your wife."
Hard: "Love your wife by... (*then figure out the 21ˢᵗ-century application and share it here*)"

Easy: *"We should* present our body as a living sacrifice."
Hard: "We can present our body as a living sacrifice by..."

Easy: *"You need to* forgive those who hurt you."
Hard: "You can forgive those who hurt you by..."

A. You-Should teachers give a quick, vague application tip, then move on

For You-Should teachers, after their explanation, they give a few quick "You should do this" or "We ought to be doing that" statements and then move on to the next point. As you would expect, they often use the Teach-and-Tip Ramblemation lesson format where they teach for a bit, give a quick You-Should tip, then move on to the next verse.

B. Here's-How teachers explain the timeless truth and demonstrate how it can be applied

On the other hand, Here's-How teachers don't move on so quickly. After explaining the text and the timeless truth that can be applied by all people of all times, they specifically explain how listeners can live out that truth as soon as they leave the church parking lot. For these teachers, it's not enough to say, "You should do this or that"; instead, they explain the truths one must believe, the attitudes one must develop, the habits one must break, the steps one must take, the changes one must make, or the actions one must perform to integrate the principles into their life.

Then, they give specific examples so listeners can 'see' how the truth applies to them. If you say, "Be honest at work," most assume they are already honest at work and would be ready to move on to the next point. However, if you give a couple of specific examples, it gives everyone a chance to reflect on their actual work ethics rather than their assumed work ethics.

For example, you may say something like this:

> We never think of ourselves as workplace thieves, but it's easy to become one just before Christmas when you're short on time and Scotch tape for wrapping presents. It's so easy to 'borrow' a roll or two of tape from the office and take it home with no real plans of returning it. Or, sometimes, we get into the practice of taking long lunches or leaving an hour early on Friday. Of course, when

payday comes, we still expect to be paid for a full 40-hour week. Most of us are honest in areas related to money, but God calls us to be honest in every area of life.

As you can see, everything changes when you give detailed, Here's-How examples that illustrate how your class can specifically apply the truths to their lives. Your lesson changes from "general abstract informational cliches meant for someone else" to "life altering, relevant truths meant specifically for each class member." The goal of your teaching is not knowledge, but to show how biblical truths fit into your listeners' lives. Don't depend on them to make the application; make it for them.

C. You-Should teachers may depend on guilt

One assumption some You-Should teachers make is that listeners don't want to obey. As a result, they feel compelled to "convince" listeners that they should, ought to, or need to obey. The more listeners appear uninterested, the more the teachers tell listeners what they "should" or "ought to" be doing; they may even throw in a few "You *really* ought to be doing this" statements.

D. Here's-How teachers depend on the Holy Spirit

Here's-How teachers, on the other hand, have somewhat the opposite view of their listeners. Their biblical perspective is closer to something like this:

As Christ followers, my listeners have a new heart and the Holy Spirit living within them. As a result, God has *already* given each one of them the *desire to obey*. Therefore, I do not need to take valuable teaching time convincing them that they should, ought to, or need to obey this or that; instead, I can concentrate on telling them *how* to obey … how to do that which they *already want* to do. I believe they want to obey and will obey as soon as they figure out how to obey. (Ezekiel 11:19; 36:26–27; Romans 12:2; Titus 3:5; Jeremiah 31:33; Galatians 6:15; 2 Corinthians 5:17; Colossians 3:9–10; Ephesians 2:10, 4:23; 2 Timothy 4:2)

Once you assume your listeners already want to live a godly life, it makes sense to spend the majority of your teaching time telling them *how* to do so.

IV. Correct, rebuke, and encourage with "great patience and careful instruction"

Now, don't misunderstand. I'm *not* suggesting listeners never need to be corrected or rebuked. They do. But even within these situations, our teaching needs to be clear, practical, and application oriented. Note Paul's teaching in 2 Timothy 4:2:

> Preach the Word; be prepared in season and out
> of season; correct, rebuke and encourage–with
> great patience and careful instruction.

Clearly, the goal, approach, and content of our preaching or teaching will vary with our particular audience. We need to "correct" those who have a wrong view of Scripture, "rebuke" those unwilling to listen and obey, and "encourage" those who will listen and obey once they know how to obey. But notice what Paul says next: no matter who you are preaching to or what its purpose is (correcting, rebuking, or encouraging), preach "with great patience and careful instruction." In short, whether we are correcting, rebuking, or encouraging, we are to do so with "great patience and careful instruction."

This means, if we "encourage" listeners to obey, but don't "carefully instruct" them on how to obey, we will only frustrate them. Likewise, if we "correct" or "rebuke" without also giving "careful instruction," then we won't deal with the root cause of the problem and it will remain in the listener's life. In order for our teaching to transform listeners' lives, we must explain the truths one must believe, the attitudes one must develop, the habits one must break, the steps one must take, the changes one must make, or the actions one must perform to integrate the principles into their life.

V. Prove that what you are saying is the same thing the Bible is saying

A. Prove that your application is biblically oriented

Of course, in your attempt to provide clear, explicit application, make sure you maintain a strong balance between explanation and application. In other words, don't swing too far the other direction by giving an abundance of application that is supported with little more than reading a verse or two. Most will consider this to be closer to advice than application.

When teachers make this mistake, they are trying to do the right thing in that they are trying to be as practical and helpful as possible. The problem is they just go too far the other direction by giving mostly application with a few verses thrown in here and there. By the end of the lesson, they may have read several verses, but they have not explained the truths and principles within the verses. They may have provided a verse to support their point, but they have not demonstrated that it actually does support their point.

As a result, because the teacher fails to show that the application is firmly rooted in Scripture, it ends up sounding more like "advice" than scriptural mandates. Then, because most listeners *don't* base their lifestyle on how the teacher thinks they should or shouldn't live, the "advice" rarely impacts life choices.

However, listeners *do* care how God wants them to live their lives. For this reason, if you can clearly demonstrate from the study that what you are saying is the same thing the Bible is saying and that your application is firmly rooted in the text, then your listeners will view it as the biblical application of the text and attempt to integrate it into their lives.

B. Proof-texting and topical teaching often lack proof

Reading a single verse to prove a point, teaching through numerous verses scattered all throughout the Bible, or trying to cover too large of a chunk of Scripture within a single lesson are all examples of teaching methods that often prevent the teacher from demonstrating that their application is firmly rooted within the biblical text.

For example, sometimes a teacher will make a point and support it with a verse in one paragraph. Then, a second point is made but supported with a verse found in a different paragraph or even in a different book of the Bible. Then, the third point, and again, it is supported with another unconnected verse. This jumping around in the Bible can prevent the teacher from spending enough time in any one passage to prove that what he or she is saying is the same thing the Bible is saying. As a result, listeners remain unconvinced that the teacher's points are biblically based, and so they rightly question any "application," or in this case, any advice given within the lesson.

Of course, I'm not saying you shouldn't incorporate verses from other places in the Bible; rather, I'm saying you need to spend enough time explaining each verse that your listeners are convinced that your point is also the Bible's point and that what you're saying is also what the

Bible is saying. However, if you make a point, then simply read a verse to support or "prove" it, then move on to the next point in the lesson, it is unlikely this proof-text will change any previously held views, beliefs, or actions. For those who already agreed with you, they will continue to agree with you, but for those who previously disagreed with you, they will remain unconvinced and continue to disagree.

Reading a verse is not the same thing as explaining a verse, and to explain a verse, you must do more than read it. This principle cannot be overemphasized! For every point I want my listeners to believe and apply to their life, I must substantiate that it is the same point the Bible is making. If I make a point my listeners don't already agree with, their first question is, "Yeah … says who?" If I don't convince them that God says so, then they will simply ignore that point. If my teaching is characterized by claims lacking biblical support, then my listeners will routinely ignore much of what I say, and my teaching will be neither informational nor transformational; instead, it will simply be viewed as Brad's thoughts and opinions.

*Reading a verse
is not the same thing as explaining a verse,
and to explain a verse,
you must do more than read it.*

VI. Exclude topics not directly related to your Sticky Proverb

A. Omit semi-related information even if it is interesting, educational, or funny

Another principle that will help you teach lessons that create doers of the Word and not hearers only is simply this: only include material that is directly related to the lesson's Sticky Proverb. Including unrelated (or even semi-related) information makes it difficult for listeners to identify the point of the lesson.

What happens is, as teachers prepare the lesson, they come across truths, insights, theological points, word studies, background information, stories, illustrations, jokes, and articles that are interesting, educational, or funny, and so they decide to include them in the lesson. However, because this information does not directly support this particular lesson's Sticky Proverb, the hodgepodge of information confuses listeners as to what point is being made.

Instead of leading the class toward a central overarching truth, the loosely related information leads the class in various directions. Remember, as you present information, your listeners are asking themselves, "What is he trying to say? What point is she trying to make with that illustration?" They are listening with the assumption that all of your information is working together to prove a particular point.

Some will conclude from your semi-related story that you are trying to make this point; others will conclude from your interesting, yet unrelated, background material that you are trying to make that point. Others will listen to your explanation of the passage, the story, and the background information and have no idea how it all fits together. At some point in their frustration, they will get distracted and begin thinking about something else.

Instead of including all you learn,
learn what to include.

B. Include that which directly supports the Sticky Proverb

What information, then, should be included and what should be excluded? What background material, word studies, theological points, or stories need to be taught in this lesson and which ones need to be saved for another day? The answer is "include only that which directly supports, explains, illustrates, backs up, or proves your Sticky Proverb."

If your Sticky Proverb succinctly states the lesson's central truth in a memorable way, then all of your lesson points should directly support it. Your Sticky Proverb is not just one of the points in your lesson; *it is THE point* of the lesson. Therefore, everything else you say should expand, explain, clarify, or illustrate this point in one way or another.

When I begin a new lesson, the first step I take is to write my Sticky Proverb at the top of the page. Then, as I write out each main point and sub-point, I check to make sure they directly support the Sticky Proverb. This is a good habit to develop since it will help you create focused M28:20 transformational lessons.

As you integrate these principles into your own teaching, your listeners are going to be excited as they learn how they can actually obey biblical principles. However, some are still going to disobey. Before assuming these individuals just don't care about obeying the now-clear principles, we need to look at one last hindrance: personal roadblocks. In the next chapter, we will look at how particular roadblocks hinder obedience in specific areas of the listener's life.

7

Remove Roadblocks

*Lead listeners around
the obstacles that hinder their growth*

*But the man who looks intently
into the perfect law that gives freedom,
and continues to do this,
not forgetting what he has heard,
but doing it—he will be blessed
in what he does.*

—James 1:25

Chapter Outline / Notes

I. **Don't assume "understanding" truth is the same thing as personally "accepting" it**

   A. Most truths make it onto the Scratchpad; fewer make it into the heart

   B. Placing truth onto the Scratchpad is easy; transferring it to the heart is hard

II. **Do roadblocks matter?**

   A. For informational teachers, "No"

   B. For M28:20 transformational teachers, "Yes!"

III. **Be willing to deal with the nitty-gritty of life**

IV. **Help listeners biblically remove roadblocks**

   A. Identify what the Bible is asking listeners to change

      1. List changes related to the head

      2. List changes related to the heart

      3. List changes related to the hands

B. Identify roadblocks that may impede this change

    1. Identify roadblocks during your preparation time

    2. Focus on gray areas people struggle with rather than black-and-white generalities

    3. Identify additional roadblocks during the lesson

C. Determine how to biblically remove each roadblock

V. Common roadblocks to be aware of

A. Unaware of how to change

B. Biblically true, but practically false

C. Procrastination, indecision, etc.

D. Comfortable with the status quo

E. Nitty-gritty life experiences

F. Group identification

VI. The house-building allegory

AS YOUR LESSONS BECOME MORE AND MORE focused and your application is built on a solid biblical foundation, you are going to find two different responses in your listeners. Some will agree with your explanation of the text and your application of its timeless truths, so they begin to integrate them into their life. Others, however, will hear and understand what you are saying, but they will *not* change.

But why?

If you will remember, earlier we looked at the difficulty of integrating biblical truths into people's lives. We saw how it is relatively easy to help them cognitively understand what is being said. However, it is far more difficult to help them move that information from their cognitive understanding to their closely guarded list of beliefs, attitudes, opinions, prejudices, views, values, priorities, hopes, dreams, and commitments. After they cognitively understand what the Bible says and how its truth can be applied, sometimes the truth stays right there in that cognitive area of their head unless we help them personally accept it and transfer it into their heart.

I. Don't assume "understanding" truth is the same thing as personally "accepting" it

People freely listen to and comprehend your lesson, but when it comes to personally accepting the truths and application as their own, sometimes a roadblock hinders the truth from moving further into their lives. It's one thing to help listeners understand truths and principles, but it's something entirely different when you ask them to personally believe it, accept it, value it, commit to it, and make it a priority in their life.

It isn't that they don't want to accept and apply the truth. They do. However, some type of challenge, painful experience, misunderstanding, justification, rationalization, or objection often blocks the truth, preventing it from moving from their cognitive understanding of it, to their heart.

A. Most truths make it onto the Scratchpad; fewer make it into the heart

In the first book in this series (*Teaching to Transform Not Inform 1: Foundational Principles for Making an Informational Sunday School Lesson…Transformational*), we looked at how it's almost as if people have a public Scratchpad in their head that is entirely different from the closely guarded personal list of beliefs, values, and opinions within their heart. Throughout each and every day, including when you teach, listeners freely place on their Scratchpad everything they hear.

B. Placing truth onto the Scratchpad is easy; transferring it to the heart is hard

However, unless listeners have a good reason to do otherwise, they keep that information right there on their

Scratchpad rather than personally believing it and transferring it to the personal and private lists they hold within their heart. Here's what seems to be true most of the time:

- Going from the Bible to one's Scratchpad is easy. Going from the Scratchpad to one's heart is hard.
- Helping listeners cognitively understand what the Bible says is easy. Helping them believe they can personally apply the truths to their own life is hard.
- Helping listeners understand how to apply the biblical truths is easy. Helping them actually integrate the truths into their life is hard.
- Listeners discuss what is on their Scratchpad but live according to what is in their heart.
- Listeners don't live according to the facts on their Scratchpad but the beliefs that reside in their heart.
- A biblically filled Scratchpad is not the same thing as a biblically filled life.

II. Do roadblocks matter?
A. For informational teachers, "No"
B. For M28:20 transformational teachers, "Yes!"

You may ask yourself, "Well, do I need to be concerned with helping listeners remove the barriers or roadblocks that hinder them from accepting biblical truths as their own?" Of course, if your goal is to be an informational teacher and you are content with simply placing information on the listener's Scratchpad, then no, you don't need to worry about the roadblocks since listeners can understand the lesson and learn the information even with the roadblocks intact. Conversely, if becoming a transformational teacher is your goal, then yes, these roadblocks are a major concern because they hinder people from integrating biblical truths into their lives.

III. Be willing to deal with the nitty-gritty of life

Helping listeners remove personal roadblocks often involves dealing with the sin, hurt, and pain in listeners' lives. Let's say you're teaching on Exodus 20:12: *Honor your father and your mother, so that you may live long in the land the LORD your God is giving you.* Simply telling your class they "should" or "ought to" honor their parents probably won't help many change. Instead, as discussed earlier, a more effective approach is to be a How-To teacher who explains how this is done in our contemporary lives. Explain what this looks like in real life. Demonstrate what types of actions are honoring and which ones are dishonoring. Before moving on, make sure your audience clearly understands *how* they can apply the principle to their life.

After you give explicit application, everyone realizes that they should honor their father and mother and they clearly understand how to do so. Unfortunately, some still won't. Hmm. Why not? Instead of assuming they just don't feel like obeying this command, look a little deeper and you will discover many reasons why some will understand but choose to disobey.

For example, some of your listeners may have had a father or mother who abandoned them as a child or was an alcoholic who abused them in one way or another. Before they can even think about honoring their parents, they will need to deal with a few overpowering roadblocks, and more than likely, they are going to need your help somewhere along the way. After all, if they could get past them on their own, they probably would have already done so ... right?

It's not that they want to disobey God. They are just having a really hard time getting around this particular barrier. They don't need you to tell them they "should" honor their parents. They already know that. And in this case, they don't even need you to tell them how to honor their parents. They know that too. What they need is for you to tell them how they can honor them despite this obstacle, that is, how they can honor parents who have abandoned or abused them.

At this point, you may be thinking to yourself, "Boy, I'm not sure I know what I would tell them. Plus, I don't think I even want to wade into that swamp. It looks a bit messy."

However, if you continue to think about it, you will realize that those who have a good relationship with their parents probably already honor them. They don't need a lesson to help them do what they are already doing. However, those who have some type of parental issue are the ones who need this lesson. Notice, the roadblock is not a lack of knowing *how* to honor one's parents nor is it a lack of wanting to obey God; rather, it relates to the nitty-gritty issues within the listener's life.

Consequently, if you're unwilling to help listeners apply Scripture within the nitty-gritty of life, there's really no reason to teach on passages like this one. After all, those who don't have any issues are already applying the truths, and those who have issues won't be helped unless you're willing to deal with the nitty-gritty life has given them.

However, if you choose to deal with life's nitty-gritty, for many, it may be the first time a teacher has actually taken the time to show them not only how to apply Exodus 20:12 but also how to apply it in the midst of their pain and suffering. I'm not saying they haven't heard numerous "you should" or "you ought to" type lessons. They have. But this may be the first time a teacher has taken the time and energy to say, "Here's how you do it in the midst of the nitty-gritty life has given you."

IV. Help listeners biblically remove roadblocks

Helping listeners remove roadblocks involves at least three steps: (1) identify what the Bible is asking listeners to change, (2) identify roadblocks that may impede this change, and (3) determine how to biblically remove each roadblock.

A. Identify what the Bible is asking listeners to change

The first step is to clearly identify what the biblical passage is asking listeners to do, start, stop, believe, commit to, value, etc. Since roadblocks directly relate to what listeners need to change, your first step is to clearly identify these changes.

Most changes relate to one of three areas: our head, heart, or hands. Changes related to the head have to do with our belief system, theology, or thought life. Changes related to our heart have more to do with our emotions, values, attitudes, or priorities. Changes related to our hands relate to our actions, whether inward or outward, public or private.

1. List changes related to the head

So, first, write down those areas the biblical text is asking listeners to change within their belief system or thought life: what they need to think, understand, learn, know, believe, disbelieve, claim, or trust. Is it asking them to believe a promise, truth, theology, or principle? Is it asking them to alter their view of something?

2. List changes related to the heart

Next, write down the areas related to the listener's psychological center that need to change, such as their emotions, values, attitudes, prejudices, priorities, commitments, choices, will, hopes, dreams, purpose, need to confess or forgive.

3. List changes related to the hands

Last, list any inward or outward, public or private, behavioral changes that need to start or stop. Are there issues to resolve, commands to obey, prayers to pray, inward or outward actions to start or stop (whether they be toward others, self, or God), offenses to forgive, new directions to take, habits to break, lifestyles to give up, or sins to confess?

Of course, many times, you will list changes in all three categories: head, heart, and hands. For example, obeying a particular biblical principle, may require a change in one's beliefs (head), values (heart), and actions (hands).

B. Identify roadblocks that may impede this change

After making a list of all the changes listeners will need to make, go back and list beside each change, potential roadblocks that may hinder listeners from integrating that particular change into their life.

1. Identify roadblocks during your preparation time

You can identify many of these roadblocks during your preparation time by simply examining your own challenges, painful experiences, misunderstandings, observations, doubts, justifications, rationalizations, and objections. Ask yourself, "Why would they refuse or hesitate to obey? Why would they fear obeying? What would cause them to procrastinate? Why might they obey, but only partially or with wrong motives?"

2. Focus on gray areas people struggle with rather than black-and-white generalities

When choosing roadblocks, look for the gray areas that hinder many rather than the obvious black-and-white generalities that block few. If you are teaching a lesson on integrity, you may correctly identify lying as a potential roadblock. The question is, which aspects of this roadblock will you focus on?

Often, our first instinct is to opt for a black-and-white generality, so we say something like this: "To live a life of integrity, we must not lie." Now, is this correct? Is lying contrary to integrity? Of course it is! But, my guess is that lying in this very general, black-and-white sense is not something most of your class does regularly. Instead, the roadblocks that prevent them from being a man or woman of integrity are the more refined forms of lying that many do not consider to be right or wrong (the gray areas that hinder them). If your goal is to be a transformational teacher who teaches individuals to obey, then these "gray areas" are the roadblocks you need to address.

Therefore, since we are surrounded
by such a great cloud of witnesses,
*let us throw off **everything that hinders**
<u>and</u> **the sin** that so easily entangles,*
and let us run with perseverance
the race marked out for us.
—Hebrews 12:1

Let's look at an example. Bob is in your class, and he has a job in marketing or sales. His customers "assume" every presentation includes "white lies" or varying degrees of "exaggeration." So, if customers naturally assume his product will only do 50 to 75 percent of what he says it will do, then, if he does not exaggerate, at least a little, he will rarely make a sale.

To make matters worse, what would happen if Bob is completely truthful while his competitors exaggerate greatly? If Bob claims half of what his competitors claim, why would anyone purchase his product? On top of that, if Bob's customers naturally assume his pitch includes the regular white lies, then they are going to assume his product is only half as good as what he stated.

So, in situations like this, is it wrong to include the *expected* "white lies" or exaggerations? If Bob's machine and his competitor's machine both make 50 items an hour, how will Bob ever make a sale when he truthfully says his machine makes 50 items an hour and his competitors claim their machine makes 100 items an hour?

These are the gray-colored roadblocks that hinder your listeners. They already know they should not lie, so telling them, "Do not lie," is not helpful. What they need is for you to show them how to apply that biblical truth to the more difficult roadblocks life places in their path.

3. Identify additional roadblocks during the lesson

It is important to realize that some issues that seem like roadblocks to you are not roadblocks to others and vice versa. In these cases, you have to allow your listeners to tell you what roadblocks you have missed. You can do this by including within your lesson, time for questions, discussion, case studies, problem solving, discussion panels, debates, role playing, and other learning activities that allow listeners to express their views.

Of course, few will directly admit their own roadblocks, so you need to find a way for them to share them indirectly. For example, when asking for feedback, ask everyone to share how they think *someone else* would object, disagree, rationalize, or differ, rather than asking them to share their own personal roadblock. Some will share what they have heard others say; others will simply share their own personal struggles.

Either way, it doesn't matter. What is important is for you to determine if there are any other roadblocks that need to be addressed within the lesson.

C. Determine how to biblically remove each roadblock

For each roadblock you identify during your preparation time, find the corresponding biblical response that will help listeners remove it. For roadblocks raised during class, if you don't know the correct biblical response, others within the class may provide it somewhere within the discussion. If no one offers a solution, simply tell the class you'll study it further and share your conclusion during the next lesson.

V. Common roadblocks to be aware of

A. Unaware of how to change

Sometimes roadblocks are related to a lack of knowledge. For example, many listeners *want* to change and *would* change if they knew *how* to change, but they don't change because they *lack the how-to knowledge* (i.e., a knowledge roadblock). This topic has been covered at great depth in earlier chapters, so I won't elaborate here other than to say, be a Here's-How teacher, not a You-Should teacher.

In your title and introduction, state the problem, issue, behavior, belief, etc., that will be addressed along with the reasons why God wants us to make the change (i.e., how the change is in our best interest, what other problems it solves, what future problems it saves us from, etc.). Then, spend adequate time telling them *how* to do what they *already want* to do.

B. Biblically true, but practically false

Another huge roadblock to be aware of is the listener's ability to believe that a passage can be both biblically true and practically false. In other words, they believe what the Bible is saying is true, yet they don't believe that applying it to their life is the best course of action for at least three reasons:

1. In their experience, the truth does not work in real life.

2. In their reasoning, the truth does not make sense.

3. In their estimation, the truth is important, but other competing truths are more important.

For example, they agree that Romans 12:18–19 tells us to live at peace with everyone and not to take revenge on those who wrong us so as to leave room for God's wrath. However, practically speaking, they don't follow that course of action for the same three reasons:

1. First, in their experience, they have found, that if they do make peace with everyone and never take revenge, then those same people take advantage of them again and again.

2. Second, this truth makes no sense to them. After all, don't you need a little backbone for people to respect you and to get things done in this world?

3. Last, there may be some value to living at peace with others, but in their estimation, being a leader, who achieves high goals, includes a degree of retaliation along the way. There just isn't time to wait on God's wrath, especially in light of the fact that God is a patient and forgiving God who may never actually right the wrong?

As you can see, your lesson will make little to no impact on your listeners until you clearly explain how Romans 12:18–19 is both biblically and practically true. Instead of saying, "So, we need to live at peace with others," and then moving on to the next verse, stop and spend several minutes addressing the reasons that hinder them from applying the verses.

I realize that, at first, you may not know how the passage connects with some of these more difficult areas of life, and it is tempting to save time by letting your class do the hard work of figuring out how to apply them. However, if you, as the teacher, do not take the time to determine how the passage applies to our lives, do you think your class will? So, if no one is making the application, what is the point in teaching the lesson?

Don't forget the principle we learned in the last book in this series, namely, "You teach more by teaching less." You teach more in the sense of bringing about more life change, by teaching less in the sense of taking time to figure out and teach how the passage is both biblically and practically true.

C. Procrastination, indecision, etc.

Other times, roadblocks relate to a heart issue. It may be that listeners know how to change and they want to change, but they lack the motivation or energy the change requires. As a result, procrastination, indecision, laziness, or other similar roadblocks hinder them from applying the lesson to their lives.

Amongst other things, you can help listeners by giving them the next single, doable, attainable step and challenging them to commit to it for a reasonable amount of time. Don't overwhelm them with twenty things to do over the next year; rather, give them one step they can take that day or that week. Of course, they are free to take all twenty steps, but you are only asking them to commit to one single step.

Encourage their God-given desire to change while reminding them that delayed obedience still reaps the consequences of sin. Show how continued disobedience affects other areas of their life they care about: their spouse, children, job, well-being, prosperity, etc. Clearly, they do not care how the sin affects the areas of their life they already know about, but when they realize the other areas and people it affects, it has a way of waking them up.

D. Comfortable with the status quo

Sometimes listeners procrastinate or disobey for an extended period of time and their passion for obedience is replaced with a contentedness with the status quo. Other times, listeners try to overcome a particular sin, but fail continuously, and they eventually give up and just accept the sin as part of their life. For these individuals, help them understand that settling for the status quo is sin and leads to a life far different than the abundant life God desires for them. Help them understand the truth of John 10:10: "The thief comes only to steal and kill and destroy; I have come that they may have life, and have it to the full."

Clearly explain how they can biblically apply the principles to their life, then challenge them to respond in faith. Be careful to avoid the use of guilt since guilt does not lead to biblical obedience. Instead, help them understand you are *on their team*, the devil and the flesh are the enemy, and you are only encouraging them to do what they already want to do. Basically, your job is to break through their complacency and say, "Hey! Listen to what the Spirit of God is saying to you in this passage!" We all need someone like that at times. Right? Be that person for them.

Stories and testimonials can also help individuals around this roadblock since they highlight how others overcame complacency and how it changed their life; how the change was worth the effort.

E. Nitty-gritty life experiences

As discussed in the last section, hardships, painful life experiences, failures, and more all have a way of hindering growth in particular areas of our life. These experiences are more difficult to determine during our preparation time, so class discussion or private conversations outside of the classroom are needed to help disclose these deep-rooted roadblocks.

F. Group identification

The last type of roadblock I want to mention relates to your listeners' desire for Group Identification. This roadblock is so camouflaged that if you are unaware of it, it is almost impossible to figure out why your listeners don't respond to your teaching. It impacts those who are motivated by a desire to belong to, be identified with, or be associated with a particular group, image, or status level. Once a person is ensnared by this roadblock, he will think, act, vote, or live in ways that connect him or associate him with the group or image in which he values.

Let's look at an example. Let's say you were teaching a lesson on tithing, and you know a businessman in your class who doesn't tithe; yet, he just bought a very expensive car and often eats at expensive restaurants.

Now, we may assume materialism is the root cause of his actions, but if we could peak inside his heart, we would discover that he's really attempting to be identified as a successful businessmen and so he's acting in ways he assumes others within this group act. Now, he may actually prefer driving a motorcycle and eating pizza at home, but since that's not what he believes successful businessmen do, that's not what he does.

One of the seniors in your class may buy the same expensive car, but her camouflaged motive is to be associated with the savvy younger generation. A teen may spend every last cent he has to buy the car, but his motive is to impress girls.

So, as you can see, in all three cases, it would be easy to assume materialism is the primary root sin, but we would be wrong. A lesson warning these listeners of materialism may have little or no impact because that's not the struggle for them. They have other issues that need to be addressed, but materialism is not one of them. It is not the roadblock hindering them from tithing.

VI. The house-building allegory

Even though many other types of roadblocks could be listed, maybe the best way to think about them is by comparing the way you would teach listeners to build their lives with the way you would teach them to build a house.

For example, if you're teaching teens, then they have lived in their house only a few years and are still in the process of building. If you told them God wants them to include another door on the first floor so they can invite more people into their life, that wouldn't be too difficult because they are still working on the first floor and haven't even begun thinking about the second floor. They just need you to be a Here's-How teacher and show them how to build the door; they will do the rest.

On the other hand, when you ask someone in their forties or fifties to make the same change, it may be a very different story. For some, they realize they must be in a constant mode of remodeling, so they integrate the change. However, for others, this is not the case. After all, not only have they completed the first floor, but they have also completed the second, third, and fourth floors, plus the roof.

Actually, they completed their house ten or fifteen years ago and are quite comfortable with its current condition (status quo). In their mind, they have some of the following roadblock-type questions that provoke them to challenge your request:

> I have successfully lived here for fifteen years, so why should I change now? If it ain't broke, why fix it? Do you realize how much that is going to cost... not to mention how long it will take? Most others don't have a second door, so why should I have to add one? What am I going to do if I add

a door to the first floor of my life, but that causes instability to the second, third, and fourth floors? What then? If they cave in a little, I'll look like an idiot. Actually, I don't think I have the ability or discipline it takes to accomplish that in the first place.

Plus, I'm not sure I want others to come in anyway. After work, I enjoy coming home and sitting in front of the TV until it's time for bed. Is there anything wrong with that? I really don't think this is as big of a deal as you are making it out to be.

Notice that the listener's questions are not a series of arbitrary questions; rather, each one relates to a core, inward roadblock that hinders them: logic, rationalizations, comparisons, self-worth, pride, reputation, discipline, and values. These are real, honest questions and objections that need a biblical response. If you don't provide answers within the lesson, listeners may not be prepared to accept the challenge you give at the conclusion of the lesson. The lesson may be informational and educational, but it will not be transformational.

This analogy also makes it easier to understand the truth behind the principle: *You teach MORE by teaching LESS.* Within a single lesson, it is pretty easy to tell everyone that they *should* add a door on this wall, replace their carpet, fix the dripping faucet, and while they're at it, add a window over the kitchen sink.

Sure, you can tell them to do all these different things, but it is unlikely they will go home and do them. For each change, not only do they have a series of "how to" questions, but they also have a long list of "why should I" questions. If you desire to teach more in the sense of bringing about more life change, you need to teach less in the sense of covering less content so you have time to answer and remove the roadblocks that hinder growth.

8

The Conclusion Challenge

*Encourage life-change by concluding
with a clear, specific, doable challenge*

*Let the word of Christ dwell in you richly,
teaching and admonishing one another
in all wisdom.*

— Colossians 3:16

Chapter Outline / Notes

I. Take time to craft the conclusion

II. Summarize the main points, application, and steps needed to remove roadblocks

III. Deliver a challenge that can be accepted
   A. Don't fear giving a challenge

   B. Encourage commitment during the conclusion

   C. Remove the option of not making a decision

   D. Be clear and specific

   E. Challenge as many different groups as possible

F. Avoid cliché challenges

G. Ensure the challenge is doable or attainable

H. Encourage them to take the next step

I. Make the commitment for a reasonable length of time

J. Include a start and stop time

IV. Give listeners time to commit

V. Last words

*L*ET'S NOW LOOK AT THE LAST SEGMENT of the Bible study lesson, the conclusion. The conclusion is important because it is where you ask listeners to make some kind of commitment to change.

Even though the conclusion can have a greater impact on the listener than any other part of the lesson, it is often one of the least prepared parts. Unprepared conclusions sound a lot like a pilot circling an airport while looking for a runway to land on. As the teacher circles the third and fourth time, you hear a few landing attempts, such as "In conclusion ... oh, yeah, also ... uh, in summary ... well, last ... that's all I have; are there any questions ... well alrighty then, let's pray." When translated, this means, "I have no idea how to end this lesson, so I'm just going to stop."

I. Take time to craft the conclusion

Of course, we all understand why developing a good conclusion is difficult—it is the last part of the lesson we prepare. By the time we get to our conclusion, we have already spent several hours studying and writing out the lesson. We are tired and ready to go to bed. It is all too easy to turn off the computer and hope the lesson's inertia will be enough to carry us across the finish line. Unfortunately, inertia-driven conclusions usually stumble across the finish line without motivating listeners to change.

A better method of motivating change within listeners is to create a conclusion that contains a summary of the main truths, a summary of how the truths can be applied, a challenge to apply the truths, and time to allow listeners to make a decision.

II. Summarize the main points, application, and steps needed to remove roadblocks

The first principle to remember about the conclusion is that it is the conclusion. It is not an additional point, but rather a summary of the main points that have already been made. Resist the temptation to throw in any informational nuggets that didn't seem to fit anywhere else in the lesson. Summarize the key points that have already been made and remind listeners of the application points along with any steps they may need to take to remove potential roadblocks.

III. Deliver a challenge that can be accepted
A. Don't fear giving a challenge

When teaching, it is easy to feel unworthy of challenging peers with the Word of God and asking them to make a commitment. We think to ourselves, "Who am I to challenge anyone?" Of course, the correct answer is, "I am no one, and if God didn't choose to work through me and you, then it may be best to just give informational lessons."

However, God does speak through us, and we are not presenting our own challenges or commands, but God's. We are simply the messenger. As long as you clearly demonstrate that the challenge is firmly rooted in the text and directed toward everyone (you and your listeners), then, if anyone gets upset (or convicted), their issue is not with you but with God. If they try to redirect their anger toward you, don't allow it by reminding them that these are God's words to us all. Step out of the way so they have to deal with God rather than fight you.

Timothy was no stranger to some of these feelings. Notice Paul's words to him:

> *Command and teach* these things. *Don't let* anyone look down on you because you are *young*, but *set an example* for the believers in speech, in life, in love, in faith and in purity.
>
> —1 Timothy 4:11–12

Paul included this exhortation to Timothy because, like us, Timothy had a few challenges that made his ministry difficult. For example, Paul had assigned Timothy to be the leader over the church in Ephesus. Now, what often happens when an authoritative figure assigns a leader to a preexisting group? Simple. People get upset and make life difficult for the new leader while trying to gain or maintain power.

Paul knew this would be true for Timothy, but that didn't stop him from telling Timothy to "*command* certain men not to teach false doctrines any longer nor to devote themselves to myths and endless genealogies" (1 Timothy 1:3–4). This church included men who were strongly moving in the wrong direction, and Timothy had to oppose them and command them to stop. It's no wonder Paul had to remind Timothy that "All Scripture is God-breathed and is useful for teaching, rebuking, correcting and training in righteousness" (2 Timothy 3:16).

Timothy did not even have age working in his favor since he was younger than many of those he was opposing. All the same, Paul exhorts him to "command and teach these things" despite feelings of intimidation, unworthiness, or inadequacy. Instead of allowing feelings to dictate actions, Paul says to "command and teach" God's Word and "set an example" in speech, life, love, faith, and purity.

B. Encourage commitment during the conclusion

Sometimes it is easier and less intimidating to skip the challenge so listeners can think about the lesson and commit on their own later, but this is not usually the best practice. Of course, exceptions always exist, but concluding with a challenge has several advantages.

At the end of your lesson, everything is fresh in their mind and clearly understood. Second, the Holy Spirit is in the process of convicting them of particular sins. If they wait a few days to respond, two things will happen: they will forget some of the finer points (or even larger points) of your lesson, and they will have quenched the Holy Spirit's work in their life.

With each passing day, they forget more of your lesson and their disobedience continues to suppress the Spirit's conviction, neither of which naturally leads to repentance.

Before they know it, it's Sunday again, and you're teaching another lesson. If you forgo another challenge, once again, they will put off making a decision, quench the Holy Spirit's work in their life, and fail to make a change. How would your teaching affect them if this pattern continued for years?

C. Remove the option of not making a decision

Once you decide to include a challenge, listeners can have a few different responses: they may decide to (1) commit to the challenge you put forth, (2) commit to a challenge they come up with, (3) make no changes at all, or (4) put off making a decision. Of these four options, you want to push them toward one of the first three. Basically, you want them to make some decision: positive or negative.

If they decide positively, then great, your lesson has helped them take the next step. If they decide negatively, then at least they have made that clear and the Holy Spirit can continue to work in that area of their life.

However, if they don't make any decision at all, then nothing has changed. They're not moving forward with a positive decision, but they haven't clearly rejected the truth either. They're in the indecisive no-man's land. You can help them out of this stagnate, indecisive state by clarifying that no decision is the same as a *no* decision and that postponing the decision is the same as disobeying. Basically, you want to remove the option of not making a decision.

*Help listeners be decisive
by clarifying that no decision is
the same as a NO decision and
that postponing the decision is
the same as disobeying.
Basically, you want to remove the option
of not making a decision.*

D. Be clear and specific

So, what challenge should you give? Sometimes it is best to let listeners determine the decision they need to make. Other times, you will specifically define the decision. Either way, give a challenge that clearly outlines *what* steps they need to take, *how* they will accomplish it, *when* it will begin, and *how long* it will last. If the challenge is vague and general (i.e., pray more, love others, be a better witness, be a godly husband, wife, father, mother, etc.), no one knows how to commit, so they don't commit. However, if the challenge is clear and specific, listeners know exactly what is being asked, and they can decide whether or not they will commit.

E. Challenge as many different groups as possible

When developing your challenge, remember that everyone may not be able to relate to it. You can avoid this problem by giving a few different challenges or a few variations of the challenge. For each lesson, consider the different groups and circumstances that exist within your class (i.e., single, single parent, married, divorced, separated, widowed, employed, unemployed, self-employed, boss, manager, handicapped, physically or emotionally impaired, elderly, rich, poor, etc.), then determine how you can expand the challenge so those within these groups can apply it to their unique situation.

Of course, you won't have time to discuss every possible situation, but the variations of the challenge will give listeners a better idea of how they can personalize and apply the truths to their own unique situation. As long as you indicate you are giving only a few of the many ways the principle can be applied, then several, clear, specific challenges usually do a better job of transforming lives than one or two vague, general ones.

F. Avoid cliché challenges

When giving a challenge, make sure it is not a cliché challenge that exhorts listeners to change some vague or intangible area of their life and contains no clear path or steps for how they would accept and accomplish the challenge. Here are a few examples I hear fairly often:

> Be burdened for the lost ... live in the power of the Spirit ... have a passion for Christ ... follow God's calling on your life ... give it to God ... get deep with God ... let God work through you ... be serious about the Great Commission ... be committed

to the church ... find God's will for your life and do what it takes to follow it, etc.

Now, everyone agrees we should do these things, but knowing how to do them is not always obvious. As a result, cliché challenges leave listeners frustrated and unchanged. It would be far more beneficial if you first asked yourself, "Exactly what would someone do to apply this truth to their life? If they are going to live in the power of the Spirit, what steps would they take?" Then, once you specifically identify what listeners need to know, believe, and do, challenge them accordingly.

Specific explicit challenges result in transformation, whereas cliché challenges only bring frustration.

G. Ensure the challenge is doable or attainable

Once you specifically know what you are going to ask listeners to do, make sure it is doable or attainable. For example, challenging everyone in your class to volunteer as a counselor for an upcoming marriage conference may be difficult for a new believer. They may lack the biblical knowledge necessary to do a good job. On the other hand, if you challenged your class to volunteer for one of the many different positions (greeter, host, information booth helper, counselor, etc.), then everyone could choose a position more suitable for their level of maturity.

Of course, some challenges by their very nature are God-sized, and without his help, they are unattainable. In this case, break the challenge down into smaller, more focused chunks, and specifically ask people to commit according to their giftedness. Help them understand that we have to trust God to accomplish through us more than is humanly possible. In addition, explain how God works through the entire body of Christ to accomplish that which no single person can accomplish by themselves.

H. Encourage them to take the next step

A point similar to the last one is this: it is often better to encourage listeners to take the next step rather than the next ten or fifteen steps. Most can take one step each week; few can take fifteen. In an earlier chapter, I gave the example of a lesson taught on love. In this lesson, the teacher taught through all thirteen verses of 1 Corinthians 13. Even though his challenges were somewhat limited in that they all related to Paul's teaching on love as found in 1 Corinthians 13, they still asked listeners to take around fourteen major steps because he gave a challenge for each of the different aspects of love as discussed in the chapter. I believe the teacher would have had a greater impact if he had focused on a couple of the aspects of love instead of all fourteen. Remember, when transformation is your goal, you "Teach MORE by Teaching LESS."

I. Make the commitment for a reasonable length of time

After giving a single, clear, explicit, doable challenge, ask listeners to commit to it for a reasonable amount of time. Instead of asking for an open-ended commitment with no beginning or ending date, ask them to commit for a couple of days or a week as opposed to months or years. Of course, once they start, they may in fact continue for a lifetime, but every journey begins with a first step. Be the one who encourages them to take it.

For example, asking everyone to commit to pray for three hours a day for one week would be unrealistic for many. Even though they may be able to pray every day for one week, many would not commit to pray each day for three hours. On the other end of the spectrum, asking them to pray ten minutes longer each day for a week would be a commitment most would be willing to make.

Transformation is not a string of weekly leaps but a progression of daily steps.

For those who rarely pray, the commitment is for only ten minutes a day for one week. For those who already pray for ten minutes a day, they would be doubling the length of their prayer time, but only by ten minutes. Still reasonable for most people. Of course, if they want to make a larger commitment, they are free to do so, but each week, listeners are able to take small steps forward because your challenges don't overwhelm them. The goal is not a string of weekly leaps but a progression of daily steps.

J. Include a start and stop time

Last, give a start and stop time. For example, you may ask them to commit to pray ten minutes longer each day, starting today and ending next Sunday before they arrive at church. Now everything is clear. Instead of asking them to "pray more," you have specifically defined what "pray more" means. They know exactly what you are asking them to commit to, the length of the commitment, when it begins, and when it ends. The ball is now in their court, and they can decide whether or not they want to commit.

IV. Give listeners time to commit

Finally, after clearly explaining the challenge, give your class enough time to make a decision. Don't ask them to think about it and make a decision sometime in the future; rather, ask them to commit one way or the other right then. Most decisions left for the future are never made, so give your listeners time to make a decision at the end of the lesson.

After giving the challenge, you can say something like this:

I'm going to close us in prayer, but first, I'm going to give you a chance to talk with God and make a decision. You may decide, "Yes, I'll commit to that," or "No, I don't want to commit right now." The important thing is to make a decision one way or another because making no decision at all is really the same thing as deciding, "No, I don't want to commit to that." Anyway, after a minute or so, I'll close us in prayer.

Then, bow your head and give them time to talk to God and make their decision. At this point, it is all right for there to be silence while they think, pray, and commit. At first, the silence may feel awkward, so resist the temptation to close in prayer after a couple of seconds.

V. Last words

Well, that wraps up this series of lessons where we looked at seven of the main ingredients that should be included in every lesson that has transformation as its goal.

1. **Sticky Proverb:** A short, memorable proverb that clearly states the passage's central truth and application.
2. **Ramblemation:** Transform lives with lessons focused on and centered around the Sticky Proverb.
3. **Captivating Introduction:** Instantly grab and hold attention by connecting listeners to the lesson's application and relevance.

4. **Visual Anchor:** The visual, concrete image, object, story, illustration, analogy, example, metaphor, testimony, or real-life situation that depicts the lesson's Sticky Proverb in a ridiculous, crazy, impossible, illogical, absurd, disproportionate, exaggerated, or animated way.

5. **Here's-How Teaching:** The thorough, applicable explanation of the biblical text that directly supports the Sticky Proverb.

6. **Roadblocks:** The challenges, experiences, misunderstandings, justifications, rationalizations, and objections the teacher helps listeners remove so they can integrate the truth into their life.

7. **The Conclusion Challenge:** Summary of the most important points and the challenge to apply them.

As you are aware, we have just scratched the surface, so I encourage you to continue to develop your effectiveness as a teacher by going through the advanced seminars where you will discover additional transformational teaching principles. As you apply these principles to your teaching, may God powerfully work through you to transform your listeners' lives and your church as a whole and thereby fulfilling the Great Commission (Matthew 28:19–20).

For additional resources and seminars,
visit www.M2820.com.

Appendix 1:
Lesson Preparation Guide

If you follow this guide as you prepare your lesson, it will remind you of the main transformational principles discussed throughout this book.

Date: _____ Lesson Passage: _____
Bible Study Series Title: _____
Individual Lesson Title: _____
                    (Titles reveal why your class should listen)
Required props, materials, resources: _____

1. Study the passage:
   A. What is the situation, conflict, event, and/or purpose of the passage?
   B. Main points within the passage:
      i.   Point 1:
      ii. Point 2:
      iii. Point 3: *(you can include additional points)*
   C. What background information, historical setting, customs, theology, etc. require an explanation?

2. Lesson's Sticky Proverb:
   A. What is the passage asking us to change *(head, heart, hands*)*?
   B. What biblical promise enables us to change?
   C. Passage's central truth or principle:
   D. Primary teaching goal and objective:
   E. Lesson's unique direction, angle, twist, or focus:

3. The Visual Anchor:

A. The visual, concrete image, object, story, illustration, analogy, example, metaphor, testimony, or real-life situation that depicts the lesson's Sticky Proverb in a ridiculous, crazy, impossible, illogical, absurd, disproportionate, exaggerated, or animated way.

4. Captivating Introduction:

A. Instantly grab attention by beginning with something surprising, novel, unusual, unexpected, unknown, mysterious, intriguing, or humorous.

B. Prove the lesson's relevance by continuing with interesting, relevant, specific, life-changing truths.

C. Show how these truths relate to the various groups** within the class.

D. Clarify what is at stake if individuals do not listen.

E. Create a huge desire to listen.

5. Here's-How Lesson:

A. Fully explain the scriptural text.

B. Show how the Sticky Proverb reflects the passage's timeless truth and application.

C. State the passage's main points in a contemporary, here's-how, relevant way.

   i. Point 1:

   ii. Point 2:

   iii. Point 3: *(you can include additional points)*

D. Make sure each point explains, supports, or illustrates the Sticky Proverb.

E. What truths need to be explained to "prove" that what you are saying is what the Bible is saying?

F. What parts of your lesson do not directly support the Sticky Proverb and need to be omitted?

6. Remove Roadblocks:

A. What are you asking listeners to change, start, stop, believe, commit to, value, etc.?
   i.   Head:*
   ii. Heart:*
   iii. Hands:*

B. Identify Roadblocks that may hinder this change (the real, possibly hidden reasons listeners disobey).

C. Answer your listeners' inner questions: *"Why should I change? How is God's plan better than my plan? What is at stake if I don't change?"*

D. What biblical promise enables or empowers them to make these changes?

E. How will you help them biblically remove these roadblocks?

7. The Conclusion Challenge:

A. Summarize the main points, application, and steps needed to remove roadblocks.

B. Give a clear, specific, doable challenge.

C. State when the commitment begins and ends. Make it for a reasonable length of time.

D. Include variations of the challenge that better relate to the different groups** in the class.

---

* The terms *head*, *heart*, and *hands* are used above to depict the broader categories, areas, or ideas listed below:

HEAD: Belief system, disbelief, thought life, insight, knowledge, view, understanding, claim/truth/faith/promise, theology, principles, learning, etc.

HEART: Emotions, hopes, dreams, purpose, values, opinions, priorities, attitudes, prejudices, will, choices, commitments, forgiveness, idols, lordship, etc.

HANDS: Actions toward others/self/God, direction, inward/outward/
public/secret activity, habits, lifestyle, discipline, confess/
repent, obedience, etc.

** Increase the effectiveness of your application, illustrations, and challenges by including a few variations of them so the different groups represented in your class can better relate to them. Below are a few of the many example groups and subgroups we all fit in.

Gender: Male - Female

Phase of Life: Child - Youth - Single - College - Newly married -
Parents - Empty nesters - Grandparents

Family Status: No prospects - Dating - Single - Married - Separated
- Divorced - Widower

Employment: Self-employed - Employed - Unemployed - Disabled
- Homemaker - First job - New job - Bored of job

Show how those in each different group can apply the lesson to their unique situations and lives.

Appendix 2: Quotations

*A Sticky Proverb is a
short, memorable, proverbial rule-of-thumb
that shows listeners how to use
biblical principles to make daily decisions.*

. . . .

*A lesson is not
the presentation of a series of related topics;
rather, it is the explanation, expansion, proof, support,
illustration, and application of the primary, central truth,
namely, the Sticky Proverb.*

. . . .

*The Sticky Proverb prevents
explanation without a destination,
arrows without a target.*

. . . .

*Before preparing or teaching,
clearly identify the God-given quest
the lesson will pursue.*

. . . .

*Without a commitment to explain, prove,
and apply a specific timeless truth,
it is easy to wander from verse to verse
displaying that which scintillates the most.*

. . . .

*A scattering of tips
is unable to explain, prove, illustrate, or
integrate any specific central point
into listeners' lives.*

. . . .

*Wandering disjointed discussions
lead to lively dialogue,
but fail to change views, beliefs and lives.*

. . . .

*Immediately connect listeners to the lesson
by sharing its interesting, relevant,
specific, life-changing truths.*

. . . .

*As the sights and smells in a restaurant
create a desire to eat,
develop a title and introduction
that creates a desire to listen.*

. . . .

*God is responsible for the substance;
we are responsible for the presentation.*

. . . .

*First, tell them **why** they should listen,
then they will be ready to hear **what**
the Bible says about the topic
that now has their interest.*

. . . .

*The goal of the introduction is NOT
to introduce the lesson, but
to create a huge desire
to listen to the lesson.*

. . . .

The goal of the introduction
is to CREATE A DESIRE TO LISTEN;
then you have the rest of the lesson
to say everything else.

....

If you want listeners to remember your lesson,
give them a picture;
if you don't mind them forgetting,
abstract truths work just fine.

....

Effective teachers constantly expand the
circle representing their teaching style
and teach outside of that circle
on a regular basis.

....

Reading a verse
is not the same thing as explaining a verse
and to explain a verse,
you must do more than read it.

....

Instead of including all you learn,
learn what to include.

....

Therefore, since we are surrounded
by such a great cloud of witnesses,
*let us throw off **everything that hinders***
*__and__ **the sin** that so easily entangles,*
and let us run with perseverance
the race marked out for us.
—Hebrews 12:1

....

175

*Help listeners be decisive
by clarifying that no decision is
the same as a NO decision and
that postponing the decision is
the same as disobeying.
Basically, you want to remove the option
of not making a decision.*

. . . .

*Specific explicit challenges result in transformation,
whereas cliché challenges only bring frustration.*

. . . .

*Transformation is not a string of weekly leaps
but a progression of daily steps.*

. . . .

Teaching to TRANSFORM Not Inform 1:
Foundational Principles for Making
an Informational Sunday School Lesson...
TRANSFORMATIONAL

People visit Bible studies they are invited to, but they join the ones that center around life-altering teaching. They join classes whose teachers are committed to making disciples, not by "teaching them the Bible," but by "teaching them to obey the Bible" (Matthew 28:20).

The series, *Teaching to TRANSFORM Not Inform*, equips teachers to change informationally or educationally oriented lessons into life-altering transformational lessons. It reveals how to teach not only the head but also the heart, which results in changed lives.

Satisfaction Guaranteed: We give a full, hassle-free, money-back guarantee for all our products. If you aren't completely satisfied, by all means, please return the item within 60 days for a prompt, courteous, and full refund. Absolutely no risks for you! Call now and get started.

Additional Resources:
• **DVD Video Companion for Teaching To TRANSFORM Not Inform Vol.1:** In this companion DVD, Dr. Simon leads your teachers through this series helping them become transformational teachers.

• **Extra Books**   (ISBN: 978-1-939257-11-6)

Get Started Today ...
To order books & DVDs for a group, see www.M2820.com for bulk pricing.

Teaching to TRANSFORM *Not Inform 2:*
How to Teach a Transformational Sunday School Lesson...
STEP-BY-STEP

In Matthew 28:19–20, Jesus gives teachers a clear and concise teaching goal: *"Therefore go and make disciples... teaching them to obey everything I have commanded you."* He did not say, teach people *what* to obey or even *how* to obey; rather, Jesus said, *"make disciples... teaching them TO OBEY."* As a result, he made life-altering transformation (not simply information or education) our primary teaching goal.

If you desire to fulfill the Great Commission through your teaching ministry, this book will place at your fingertips a simple, practical, step-by-step process for how you can teach life-altering lessons that use information and explanation to bring about transformation in your listeners' lives.

Additional Resources:
• **DVD Video Companion for Teaching to** TRANSFORM **Not Inform Vol.2:** In this companion DVD, Dr. Simon leads your teachers through this series helping them become transformational teachers.

• **Extra Books**   (ISBN: 978-1-939257-21-5)

Get Started Today ...
To order books & DVDs for a group, see www.M2820.com for bulk pricing.

Host a Live Training Event

If you are interested in hosting a live *Teaching to TRANSFORM Not Inform* training seminar for teachers in your church and/or area, visit www.M2820.com and request additional information.

Each seminar can be tailored to fit the specific needs of your church or group.